CONTENTS

Foreword by Wyatt Flores	4
Prologue (Why I Wrote This Book)	8
The Boys From Oklahoma	14
The Turnpike Troubadours	24
The Price of Admission	30
The Great Divide	36
Jason Boland and The Stragglers	42
Stoney LaRue	48
Oklahoma Breakdown: The Mike Hosty Story	54
I Am Trying to Break Your Heart	62
Grady Cross	70
Randy Ragsdale	78
Jeremy Plato	86
Cody Canada	92
Night One	100
Night Two	120
Night Three	140
Night Four	160
Epilogue (Standing in the Afterglow)	180
Last Word by Kaitlin Butts	188

Foreword

Just being a fan is where Red Dirt started with me.

When I was old enough that I could go see concerts, that became the turning point. I started going to Red Dirt shows, and it all started to change for me. Before that, I just played guitar for fun. Once I started going to shows, instead of singing along or dancing, I started studying. I studied all that the band was doing and tried to figure it out. I'd watch what the guitar player was doing. That's when it all changed. That's when my perspective changed.

As a fan, I loved the music. I loved the stories. I knew what they were talking about. It was right here in Stillwater. This is my backyard. But, as I got into the professional side of things, that's when I started trying to figure out: *How am I going to be the next thing that comes out of here? Do I have what it takes to make it out? I know I'm a Red Dirt artist, but how do I go play everywhere?*

Well, it worked for me. It's not like I tried to form my songwriting into something that would be heard by everybody. I just told my truth. That got me all the way around the world.

The Great Divide had a huge impact on that. Not only was it the personal relationship that I had with Scotte (Lester) and Kelley (Green) — Kelley is pretty much like my second dad, and I'd call Scotte the same, but he's really more like our uncle — but it was them sitting down and teaching me songs. They were always trying to push me to keep on playing and to learn things. I was just lucky enough to have

NEVER SAY NEVER NEVER SAY NEVER
SAY NEVER SAY NEVER SAY NEVER SAY
NEVER SAY NEVER SAY NEVER SAY NEVER
SAY NEVER SAY NEVER SAY NEVER SAY
NEVER SAY NEVER SAY NEVER SAY NEVER
SAY NEVER SAY NEVER SAY NEVER SAY
NEVER SAY NEVER SAY NEVER SAY NEVER
SAY NEVER SAY NEVER SAY NEVER SAY
NEVER SAY NEVER SAY NEVER SAY NEVER
SAY NEVER SAY NEVER SAY NEVER SAY
SAY NEVER SAY **NEVER SAY NEVER** SAY
NEVER SAY NEVER SAY NEVER SAY NEVER
SAY NEVER SAY NEVER SAY NEVER SAY
NEVER SAY NEVER SAY NEVER SAY NEVER

CROSS CANADIAN RAGWEED, THE BOYS FROM OKLAHOMA, AND A RED DIRT COMEBACK STORY FOR THE AGES

This book is dedicated
to our alma mater, O-S-U.

Copyright 2025 Back Lounge Publishing | Josh Crutchmer

All rights reserved. Published in 2025

No part of this book may be reproduced, stored in a retrieval system,
or transmitted in any form by electronic or mechanical means
without prior written permission from the author.

ISBN-13: 979-8-9928554-1-8

All copyrighted material included in this publication has been used by permission.
All research and reporting is original except when noted. Any errors that may have occurred
in are inadvertant and will be corrected in future printings, provided notification is sent to
the author. All photography is original to the author except where credited.

Book editor: Andrea Hancock | Editorial consultant: Andrea Zagata.

Book design and cover design: Josh Crutchmer.

Back cover: Cross Canadian Ragweed performs on the first night of The Boys From Oklahoma.

Back cover photo by Clay Billman.

Never Say Never logo and artwork created by Josh Crutchmer.

This book supports Okmulgee Family YMCA. Learn more at ymcatulsa.org/okmulgee.

neversayneverbook.com | crutchmer.com

FOREWORD

them in my life, where I could ask them questions, and I was just fascinated by it all. When it comes to their actual music, Mike McClure is someone who I believe to be one of the best songwriters in the world. I could sit here and listen to all of their albums. They are so diverse, yet you always know it's them. Their sound changes over time, but they are still The Great Divide, if that makes any sense. I just love going through their albums and hearing the different styles they bring out, because that is what heavily influenced everything about my music.

When I watch The Turnpike Troubadours play — you can hear this on their albums, but you can really see this live — it's how they use their instruments to fill in all the gaps. Their dynamics are incredible. I focus on so much of that in my own music, the way they can get so quiet and then come back up and be so loud. I try for that dynamic myself — to have music that is so easy to listen to, that isn't so busy, while *still* being busy. Turnpike is always adding all the right licks in all the right spots. But it's always simple music that is simple to understand. It's easy to hear the entire story in a Turnpike song. It's easy to latch on to, and that's what I keep trying to do. The hard part, for me, is in their songwriting, because all that I aspire to do is to write songs as good as Evan Felker. Not only is it that it's a great melody and a great idea for a song, but it's actual storytelling. I am still trying to figure that out. I know that my music has done great so far, but that is what I am inspired to be — to write those stories that are fully thought-out, and tell a full tale, and do it in a short amount of time. There's a word economy in those songs, where I know exactly what you're talking about. I see the picture you are painting immediately.

Trying to get that down in my own songwriting is where Turnpike influences me. That's *why* Turnpike is Turnpike.

It all starts with the song, and good Lord, do they have songs! I couldn't show you a bad one in their catalog. They stick so true to songwriting, and then, when they come together as a band, it adds everything else they need.

I am getting emotional thinking about Cross Canadian Ragweed, because of how many times I have been driving around on these dirt roads. Most people still don't realize that, when I say I am from here, I truly mean that this is my backyard, and these are the roads that I drive. It's more than just saying I am from here or that I went to col-

NEVER SAY NEVER

lege here — especially because I did not! I went to OSU-IT in Okmulgee, an hour and a half away. So, when I saw them sing "17," and I saw 40,000 people screaming that song, I still don't have the words to even describe the feeling I had. But, all those times I drove those dirt roads or that I sat in the middle of this town going, "I don't know what I'm gonna do, but when I graduate, I'm gonna get out of here," only to find that all I wanted to do was come home — of course, that was what my album *Welcome to the Plains* was about — I really know how it feels to always be 17 in my hometown.

People still come up to me and bring up the old days, and they still see me as that kid here, even though I've changed so much.

And, I want to do what Ragweed and Turnpike have done. I do want to go down as one of the great songwriters to come out of Oklahoma. Am I there yet? No. Do I want to be there? Absolutely. When I watched everyone get inducted into the hall of fame, I wanted to do that. I want to be a part of the greats in this scene.

However, more than anything, what I don't believe I have done, but what I think they have just done — that I wanted to see done — is *light this town on fire again.*

The amount of music that is here over these four days at The Boys From Oklahoma is absolutely insane. The amount of artists that are here is insane. This is the biggest weekend that I think Stillwater has ever had. And it's because the scene itself is slowly starting to die off. When I go down to The Strip, I don't see that many live bands. It's all clubs starting to pop up now. Yes, there are great bars for that, but what this town was built off of was Red Dirt, and I wish that would come back. I wish that community would come back. I know Stillwater has the spark; it has just been a little dim over the years.

I want to see this town back to where every place you go, you can see live music, and you don't know who's going to play or what to expect. I hope all of this starts that scene up again. I hope this is the spark, and I hope that I get to be a part of it.

And, I am honored that these bands asked me to come play with them this weekend. I would have been just as happy to go sit in the stands and watch. But it means the world to me that they are letting me come out there and join them — in all this.

Wyatt Flores, April 2025

FOREWORD

NEVER SAY NEVER

Why I Wrote This Book (the Prologue)

William Dyer made it maybe 30 minutes into his first Cross Canadian Ragweed concert before, at least to him, my jig was up.

This was Saturday night, April 12, 2025, in the wings of a massive stage occupying the east end zone of Boone Pickens Stadium on the campus of Oklahoma State University in Stillwater, Oklahoma. For the past year and a half, Dyer has been fascinated by me. More specifically, he's been fascinated by my ties to the Red Dirt music scene that began half a century ago, less than two miles from where he and I were standing. Dyer was taking in the Ragweed show — the third of four concerts in four nights that Ragweed co-headlined with The Turnpike Troubadours, dubbed "The Boys From Oklahoma" shows.

I was talking to Wyatt Flores, the 23-year-old Stillwater native and Red Dirt prodigy who will formally kick this book off one chapter from now, about the spectacle of the night. Flores was raised on Red Dirt, but he'd never seen anything like this. Before Ragweed went on, Turnpike had already put on one of the most memorable single concerts this state had ever seen — including guest appearances from Flores, Molly Tuttle, and Ketch Secor of Old Crow Medicine Show — putting the 48,000 strong in attendance through the wringer with their stomping, hard-country live show. Now, Ragweed was playing to those same 48,000, and they were putting on a rock show. The swampy, swinging, fiddle-and-steel Troubadours show gave way to Ragweed's elec-

PROLOGUE

tric, sweaty extended reunion set that somehow managed to feel both brand new and like a ride in a time machine. Flores and I were simply taking it all in. The most we'd said to one another was, "I can't believe this is real."

But Dyer, who hails from Tennessee, was adopted into Red Dirt barely two years prior when he signed on to co-manage Flores (along with Braden Milford). Dyer had spent a great deal of his free time in those two years reading my writing, doing his best to educate himself on Red Dirt. He'd been through my 2020 book, *Red Dirt*, and its late-2024 sister, *Red Dirt Unplugged*, enough to have the scene figured out. Dyer had seen Turnpike at least half a dozen times by then. But now, watching Ragweed captivate the stadium with unbridled, in-your-face rock and roll, he decided to call me out.

"You're telling me this is Red Dirt?" he asked.

"Yeah," I said.

"And … Turnpike is *also* Red Dirt?"

"Yeah."

"Well, I am definitely more confused about what Red Dirt is than when I got here. You're falling asleep on the job!"

Just like that, my Red Dirt invincibility faded, right there in front of everybody. I had zero answer as to how a small-town cowboy like Turnpike frontman Evan Felker and a pot-smoking hippie like Ragweed's leader Cody Canada can be the two faces of a single genre, but there they were, taking turns captivating a stadium, a city, and a whole state. William, I'm sorry. I don't know how Red Dirt can be that country and that rock at the same time, I just know that you saw it with your own eyes, and now you can never go back to the person you were before the sun went down that night. But you're in good company, because neither can I.

I said in *Red Dirt Unplugged* that I learned about Ragweed's plans to reunite after a 15-year hiatus back in August of 2024. I was at the Braun Brothers Reunion in Challis, Idaho, sitting on a blanket in the grass watching Wade Bowen headline the second of the three-night festival in this tiny mountain town. Shannon Canada — manager of both Ragweed and Cody Canada and The Departed, and Cody Canada's wife — tapped me on the shoulder and said, "Crutch. He's doing it," and I was so far into my acceptance that we'd never see Ragweed play again that I had no idea what Shannon was telling me. A full five minutes passed before I did a slapstick double-take, to Shannon's great amusement.

When I composed myself, all I said was, "You know I'm gonna be writing about that, right?"

Shannon nodded.

Six months earlier, I had profiled Canada in *Rolling Stone* — which is not my employer, by the way. That title goes to *The New York Times*, where I'm the planning editor — and the headline read, "Cody Canada Is Reviving a Cross Canadian Ragweed Classic Album — But Says the Band Will Never Reunite." Ostensibly, we were talking about The Departed's re-recording of Ragweed's seminal *Soul Gravy* record, but really, we were talking about Ragweed. Cody said "never." Now, here was Shannon, telling me that word had a shelf life after all.

The first time I got to speak to Canada on the record was in September of 2024, on his tour bus in his hometown of New Braunfels, Texas. Within a minute, he got to the heart of the matter and that now-obsolete headline.

"Never say never," Cody said, with the kind of smirk you used to crack when you were a kid and got caught rummaging through the snack drawer before dinner.

What I am saying is, this book is about to write itself.

I started researching it before *Red Dirt Unplugged* was even released, holding back interviews and making notes that I intended for that book. By April of 2025, I had interviewed all the members of Ragweed — Cody Canada, Grady Cross, Randy Ragsdale and Jeremy Plato — and had a long talk with Evan Felker, too. For good measure, I did the same with the rest of the artists on The Boys From Oklahoma bill: The Great Divide, Jason Boland and The Stragglers, and Stoney LaRue.

But I held back on writing it until April. You're reading that correctly. This book was written, in its entirety, over two-and-a-half weeks in the run-up and afterglow of the four concerts at Boone Pickens Stadium. The final four chapters in this book were written following each of the four shows.

One more thing that is pretty important at the outset: I did not intend this book to be a historical essay on Ragweed and the bands playing these concerts. The primary reason is, every band on The Boys

PROLOGUE

From Oklahoma bill got a chapter in *Red Dirt* that breaks down their history and influences. Most of them — The Divide especially — got a reprisal in *Red Dirt Unplugged*. I wanted to write *Never Say Never* in the moment and of the moment. There will be plenty of times in this book where history and biographies take center stage, most often in the form of an artist's own recounting of what got us to this point, but I am trying throughout this book to place us in April of 2025 as much as I can.

There are also some moments from the run-up to The Boys From Oklahoma that I have previously detailed for Rolling Stone and my own Back Lounge site that will be referenced time and again in this book. The most significant ones were the six-song performance by Cross Canadian Ragweed at the 2025 Mile 0 Fest in Key West, Florida, at the end of a Ragweed tribute set from festival performers. That marked Ragweed's official first public performance since 2010. The other was the surprise induction of Ragweed into the Oklahoma Music Hall of Fame on March 1, 2025 — which involved me surprising Cody Canada and The Departed on stage at Cain's Ballroom with the news and inviting members of the hall of fame up to make it official. Ragweed also played a six-song encore that night at Tulsa's Timeless Honky-Tonk. The next week, the hall also surprised The Great Divide, Jason Boland and the Stragglers, and Stoney LaRue with the news they would be joining Ragweed as members.

I don't want you to have my best-written, refined prose. I want you to have this book. I want it in your hands while the memory of The Boys From Oklahoma is living and breathing in your mind, in color and surround sound. I'm happy to sacrifice months of editing and refining if I can capture the feeling inside that stadium while it's still there for the capturing. I'm going to write it conversationally, as much as I can as if we were discussing these shows over cheese fries at Eskimo Joe's in Stillwater. The tenses may change and the subjects and verbs may not agree, but that's a trade I am willing to make.

I'm a journalist, not an author. I live and breathe on deadlines. I have produced massive newspaper special sections the morning after a major sports championship or breaking news event. That was my reflex when I first heard about The Boys From Oklahoma — write an entire book about it, and write it immediately.

NEVER SAY NEVER

Here you go. I hope you like it.

I'm really sorry to Andrea Hancock, who I tasked with editing this project, but she's a journalist, too. I think she will understand. I am also grateful to her for her edits, and that's a great transition from "why I wrote this book" to "here's my list of people to thank."

I am eternally indebted to the Canada family: Cody, Shannon, Dierks, and Willy. Same goes for Cross, Ragsdale, and Plato. Evan Felker, and all of Turnpike, once again welcomed me into their circles for this project. Catching up with The Great Divide, Jason Boland, and Stoney LaRue is something I never do as much as I'd like. Separately, a veritable army of enablers worked to make this happen: Jon Folk, Russell Doussan, Darren Shrum, Shooter Jennings, Kyle Carter, and anyone else who spoke on the record; Kyle Waters, Chad Weiberg, and everyone at OSU; Katie Dale and Ashley Kirkley at the Red Dirt Relief Fund; Stan Clark and Tim Holland at Eskimo Joe's; Marci McDaniel, Allie Sisioan, Brandy Reed, Paddy Scace, Andrew McInnes, Carla Sacks, Joe Sivick, Mark Noel, Brian Kinzie, Chris McCoy, Willard Kendall, Nelson Reuwer, and anybody else who showed me the ropes, pointed me to a setlist, or let me hang around in any capacity. Then there are just as many people away from the microphones who propped me up for this project: Andrea Zagata, Annemarie Lopez, Jake Lopez, Wes Crutchmer, and Andie Hancock (you told me that you're "Andie" when I am referencing my friend). My group chat sounding boards are always Dean Stiffler, Merylee Stiffler, Jimmy Flex, Kari Flex, and Lori Hillhouse. Then there are Katie McElhaney and Kaylee Vaughn, who are letting me partner with the Okmulgee Family YMCA, the first time any of my projects has ever benefited my hometown — Okmulgee, Oklahoma — directly. Also, Tom Jolly and my *New York Times* bosses let me do this, and Joe Hudak and his *Rolling Stone* colleagues amplify it exponentially. And finally, one huge thank you is due to Wyatt Flores and Kaitlin Butts for contributing their own words to kick this whole thing off and wrap it up.

Now let's turn these pages into one big rock room. Or honky-tonk. Or both.

It's all Red Dirt in the end.

PROLOGUE

NEVER SAY NEVER

The Boys From Oklahoma

The legacy of The Boys From Oklahoma shows, ultimately, will be their sheer scale. At a time when music festivals are scaling back, or shuttering altogether, a four-day music festival in Stillwater drew nearly 200,000 people to the college town on the Oklahoma plains.

From the start, that scale never actually set in with Cody Canada. For all the credit Cross Canadian Ragweed gets for exposing the world to Red Dirt, it spent the arc of its career as a bar band. Canada's current band, The Departed — featuring Canada, Jeremy Plato on bass and drummer Eric Hansen — is still a bar band. Coming back, suddenly, as a stadium act is barely comprehensible to the Ragweed frontman.

"We got into Stillwater on Monday night, and kind of had the keys to the kingdom," Canada says ahead of the show. "We walked around everywhere, and man, you can look at it all you want to on a piece of paper, but good Lord, it's big. I've been to so many shows like this, but I've never done it."

The subtext to that legacy, regardless of how silly the thought seems in hindsight, is how unlikely the whole thing was in the first place.

A year ago, the idea of a reunion residency at this scale would have been laughable. Ragweed's final show, in October 2010 at Joe's Sports Bar in Chicago, followed a year of internal turmoil that left hard feelings and bitterness in the band. In February 2024, Canada ruled out a comeback, to me, in a story that landed in *Rolling Stone*.

THE BOYS FROM OKLAHOMA

In truth, however, the notion had been on Canada's mind for nearly two years. He saw the fervor that followed Turnpike's 2022 reunion after a three-year break, and social media comments suggesting that Ragweed should be next. Jon Folk — agent for both Ragweed and The Departed, as well as Turnpike — had steadily fielded offers since Ragweed broke up, but he started receiving the kind that crept into life-altering territory. Canada started running the idea of a comeback past his peers. Robert Earl Keen told him to take a victory lap. Great Divide frontman Mike McClure told him that Canada would feel like a weight had been lifted.

"To be able to reconcile that, and to think about how happy this is going to make their fans," McClure says, "I really can't believe it."

The road to The Boys From Oklahoma, in hindsight, was less of a road and more of a tightrope — but only one that could have been understood to be a tightrope at the end of it all.

The tightrope began at Oklahoma State University. Right about the time Canada was swearing off a comeback, Darren Shrum was dreaming big. At the time, the university president was Kayse Shrum. Darren is her husband. And in early 2024, he thought bringing concerts to OSU's athletic facilities would help fill a need for name, image, and likeness money for the program. He ran the idea past Kayse. "She said, 'Go for it,'" Darren recalls.

Darren Shrum was envisioning a series of concerts at Gallagher-Iba, OSU's 13,000-seat basketball and wrestling arena. He took the idea to Kyle Waters, the university's athletic director for facilities. Waters responded by sharing a years-old proposal he had made for a concert at Boone Pickens Stadium. Waters once briefly worked for Coachella, and it gave his vision some heft.

"I told him, 'Kyle, I've known you for a long time. Why have you never said anything about this to me?' And he said, 'I didn't think it would matter, because I didn't think I'd ever see a concert in Gallagher-Iba or Boone Pickens Stadium,'" Darren recalls.

With permission to move forward, Darren — along with Waters and director of football business Kenyatta Wright, a former Oklahoma State and NFL player who is close with Turnpike — started brainstorming. They wanted a country show to be the first one. They contacted Russell Doussan, whose company, Doussan Music Group, is currently producing and promoting Alan Jackson's Last Call Tour. With Doussan's help, OSU put an offer out for a concert featuring Jason Aldean and Miranda Lambert co-headlining. But, Darren says, more than a month passed without an answer. "I told him, 'Kyle, we've gotta do something different,'" he says.

That's when Waters suggested asking Ragweed.

"I said, 'Can they fill the stadium?' And Kyle said, 'I don't know, but I think so,'" Darren recalls. "So I said, 'We're gonna push forward.'"

Waters may have been taking a guess, but it was a highly-educated one. Both Waters and his brother, Trey, were bartenders at the Wormy Dog Saloon at the turn of the millennium when Ragweed would play there once a month for a $3 cover at the door. The odds of the person wielding the greatest control and influence over what became The Boys From Oklahoma being someone who was there when Ragweed were little more than local heroes were astronomical on their own. Add in his real-world Coachella perspective, and Waters became lightning in a bottle in his own right, as far as these shows are concerned.

They contacted Folk, who contacted Canada. This time, the thought of a comeback stopped Canada cold.

"I think there were some unresolved feelings around when and how the band split up," Folk says. "All the guys in the band had regrets over how that chapter ended. I've always found that in life that time heals all wounds. If you were around back in the Ragweed era, you know how much fun their show was and how much happiness it brought to everyone in the room.

"Ultimately, I think after years of arguing with himself, Cody woke up one day and said, 'I'm tired of being upset about this, and I'm going to do something about it.'

"He told me, 'If the guys are up for it, I'd love to add some more chapters to our story.'"

Folk reached out to Grady Cross and Randy Ragsdale separately.

Cross's mind didn't go to Ragweed; it went to his kids. His daughter, Charlie, and son, Slaid, were young when the band broke up. Slaid is 19 now, and he plays guitar in a hard-driving country band called The Smokin' Oaks, based in Yukon, Oklahoma. Canada has two sons, Dierks and Willy, who are in their late teens. They play in Waves in April, a metalcore band based in New Braunfels, Texas.

Cross saw a chance for the band to show their children what their old men were capable of together.

"It's everything," Cross says. "We were gone a lot, and when we broke up, we went home and raised our kids. They're at the age now where they get to do fun stuff. But Instagram wasn't around when we played. They never got to see what we were like. This really is everything."

Cross and Ragsdale said yes, and a deal was made.

Almost immediately, it became clear that the notion they may never get to do it again was an overly-cautious one. The ticket presale window revealed a massive demand for a Ragweed concert. One night became four nights, and a public on-sale never happened at all.

With that as the background, Folk, Doussan, and Shrum all spoke with me on the record for this book and for the *Rolling Stone* story on the reunion that ran the morning after the first show. What follows are excerpts from the interviews we held.

Jon Folk

From your perspective, how did these concerts come together?
Over the past eight or nine years, Cody and I have had many "late night" conversations about the possibility of a Ragweed reunion, but I never wanted Cody to feel pressure from me or any outside party. I think he appreciated having someone to talk to about it who wasn't going to hound him to reunite for the wrong reasons. If he would have just done a money grab reunion show, he would have regretted it for the rest of his life.

Additionally, he was and is thriving with The Departed, thriving on the road, making a great living, touring nationally.

But, deep down, I think there were some unresolved feelings around the when/how the band split up. All the guys in the band had regrets of how that chapter ended. I've always found that in life, time heals all wounds, and if you were around back in the Ragweed era, you know how much fun a Ragweed show was — and how much happiness it brought to everyone in the room.

What they accomplished as independent artists changed the music business back then and what they have accomplished now has once again changed the business. Ultimately, I think after years of arguing with himself, Cody woke up one day and said, "I'm tired of being upset about this and I'm going to do something about it." He said, "If the guys are up for it, I'd love to add some more chapters to our story."

Why do you think that now was suddenly the right time for them?
The reality is, whether this reunion was a one-night stand at Eskimo Joe's or four sold-out nights at Boone Pickens Stadium, *now* is the right time, because they aren't doing this for any other reason than love of the band, love for each other, love for the fans — old and new — love of the music, and the chance to add a couple of more chapters to the story of Cross Canadian Ragweed.

Now that the shows are upon us, are you still as excited for them as you were back in October when they were announced?
Shoot, October was just when they were announced! Hell, the planning of this goes back *way* longer than that. You know how hard it was to keep this a secret?

Honestly, to answer your question, "excitement" doesn't even come *close* to what I'm feeling.

Just like everyone else in the stadium, first and foremost, I'm there as a fan. I am going to be reliving one of the best times in my life. Red Dirt music truly changed my life, and I've spent 25 years promoting this music literally around the world. This music and business *is* my life because of these acts!

Seeing Boland, Stoney, The Great Divide, Turnpike, and Ragweed on this big of a stage? Are you kidding me? I'm in! These guys defined Red Dirt, and I'll be down in the pit or up in the stands every night along with 183,000 others, singing along with the bands.

Russell Doussan

How did you first come on board to The Boys From Oklahoma shows?
When Jon Folk informed me about the potential of a Ragweed reunion after 15 years, I suggested this idea of a Stillwater launch, using OSU and Boone Pickens Stadium as the venue. We began working through the logistics with the university and the bands — and, ultimately, this became a true partnership.

How are you viewing the shows, now that they are upon us and the hype is a thing of the past?

I am still in the "Is this real?" mode. Again, being in this business for almost 31 years, and having worked with many level-A artists and massive events, I have *never* been a part of something so explosive. From the first tease of a CCR reunion, through the four sold-out on-sale days, into the week of the event, it's just special on so many fronts. The work effort from all the teams involved has been incredible.

I cannot wait to enjoy the shows ... hoping to be able to also be a "fan" at some point!

Darren Shrum

As you recall, what spurred these concerts? Where did the idea originate?
The whole reason that this concert idea was even brought to life was out of necessity, for NIL (the name, image, and likeness programs for Oklahoma State athletics). My plan was to put together a spring concert and a fall concert, hoping we could raise a bit of money and then do a few other types of fundraising events. I wanted to help show that the university was doing its part, since we have donors giving us money too.

So I was talking to Kayse last January — over a year ago — and just said, "Hey. I've got this idea." She goes, "That sounds like a great idea, and you know we need the money. Go for it."

I had the vision, and I had the "yes" — which was the most important thing to have — and I immediately went over to see Kyle Waters. I said, "I need a floor plan of Gallagher-Iba," and he goes, "Darren, they're not gonna do it." And I look at him like, "We're not asking permission, Kyle. We've got permission. We're going for it, and we're moving forward."

Well, he had this plan he put together several years ago in hopes that they would do something. I still have that original plan now, and it showed us we could seat between 40,000 and 45,000 people [at Boone Pickens Stadium]. I saw it, and I said, "Dude. This is freaking awesome. Now, do you have any idea where we get started?"

We start talking about contacts, and he tells me he was with Coachella for several years. I'm going, "Dude. I've known you for a long time. Why have you never said any of this?" And he tells me it's because he never thought it would matter, that he never thought he'd see a concert in Gallagher-Iba or Boone Pickens. And I said, "In my hopes and dreams, we're going to see one at every venue here at Oklahoma State, maybe even at the baseball field."

Kyle says, "I'm all in."

What was the bridge between that and The Boys From Oklahoma?
At some point in early spring 2024, Kyle reached out to Russell at DMG. He had known him, I think, from Coachella, and he gave him a call. He comes back with a lead on, potentially, a big concert with big names — Miranda Lambert and Jason Aldean. We kind of went with that for a while.

Well, my father was actually sick then. He passed away last July 4th, and all this happened back in the spring, right? So, I wasn't getting to talk to Kyle much. I used to stop in his office two or three times a week just to say hey, and that wasn't happening. Well, after maybe 30, 45 days of not hearing anything on that original plan, I reached out and started pushing him: "Dude. We've got to have *something*. We've got nothing in writing. We've gotta do something different."

That's when Kyle said, "Let me call Shannon Canada."

Her first answer was, "Cody says, 'No. We'll never get back together.'" At least, those were Kyle's words to me after they talked. And I thought that sounded like a hard "no" and I wanted to keep digging. We had started getting offers for a spring show, but at the time, I was pushing for something in the fall.

Well, not long after that, Kyle calls me and he says, "Shannon and Cody want to talk again," and I tell him to let me know how it goes.

He calls back and goes, "They're going to consider it."

"No shit? That's awesome!"

But then, my biggest question was, "Kyle, can they fill the stadium? We've gotta be at 32,000 tickets to break even."

Kyle says, "Let's just push forward and see what happens."

Then, at some point, they agreed to do it.

Once you have an agreement, and the parameters are worked out, how do you feel once you see word get out and it turns into the biggest concert event in state history?
I started watching social media — and I only get on Instagram and X on occasions — and I see this post, maybe a month out, or a few weeks out. It was just velvet on the Ragweed page. They didn't do any other posts.

And I start seeing all these people responding to it. So I call Kyle, and I'm all giddy. I said, "I'm getting kind of nervous, in a good way. I'm getting a little excited," and he goes, "Man. I can't sleep."

We're like six weeks out from the first tickets on sale, and they post "2025" on their website. Well, I'm on the visitors board, and we start to see hotels get snatched up. Kyle goes, "Man. We've gotta keep this quiet," and I'm like, "Dude, I haven't told *anybody*."

We get to the day of the presale, and Kyle and I are just sitting there watching and listening, and just going, "Holy shit." I think we sold out in 15 minutes, even though people were still posting, "I wish my little green guy would run faster."

We immediately sell out two shows, right?

So, I call Kayse, and I go, "Hey, what about a Thursday show and a Sunday show?" And she says she wants to verify it's OK with the provost.

So, she called (Vice Provost of Undergraduate Education) Jeanette Mendez and said, "What do you think about Thursday, as far as how it is going to impact school?"

Jeanette says, "Well, we've done Thursday night football games before, yeah?"

So Kayse jokingly says to me, "Let's just call it Stilly-Stock and shut down campus for a week."

Well, I went ahead and *proposed* that to Russell!

Well, Turnpike had some other things on the schedule, either on the Wednesday or the Monday, so we called it at four nights, and that's the story.

We had Russell down for a football game last fall, and I just went, "OK. Did you ever think this was gonna be possible?"

And he goes, "Hell no. This was lightning in a bottle."

The Cross Canadian Ragweed band, crew and family at The Boys From Oklahoma. (Todd Purifoy)

THE BOYS FROM OKLAHOMA

NEVER SAY NEVER

The Turnpike Troubadours

"**M**usic, to me, is Turnpike Troubadours," Evan Felker says. "That's all that music is to me. That's the only band I've ever been in. That's the only thing I've ever done. Other than a weekend here and there, that's the only way that I've ever been on stage that was *real* to me. This band has been my crowning achievement in life, other than having kids and a family."

Felker is speaking ahead of The Boys From Oklahoma concerts, where the Turnpike Troubadours are co-headlining with Cross Canadian Ragweed in Stillwater.

As a genre, Red Dirt is at its peak in the world's musical eye right now. Getting to this moment, however, involved a series of smaller peaks. There was The Great Divide's mid-1990s rise and subsequent Atlantic Records deal. That was followed by Ragweed's extended heyday that started around 2002 and lasted until their 2010 breakup. Ragweed's break coincided with Turnpike's rise and Red Dirt's third peak. By the time the 2020s rolled around, the post-pandemic world was clamoring for live music, and Turnpike was waiting. Their own return from a hiatus in 2022 resulted in the kind of off-the-charts demand for tickets that the world usually reserved for such mainstream A-listers as Taylor Swift or Beyoncé.

Inadvertent though it may have been, Turnpike's comeback laid the groundwork for Ragweed's. When 70,000 fans jammed the ticket queue for Turnpike's 2022 reunion at the 1,700-capacity Cain's Ballroom in Tulsa, it showed Jon Folk — who books both Turnpike and Ragweed for William Morris Endeavor — just what potential bands at the top of Red Dirt suddenly had. When Ragweed got back together, it allowed him to scale up his own expectations and dream of a show at Boone Pickens Stadium.

But if Turnpike enabled Ragweed, they were simply returning the favor. Two decades ago, Felker and Kyle Nix found themselves living in Stillwater, plying their own trade in the bars around town and hoping to follow the trail that Ragweed had blazed out of Stillwater and into real, sustainable success. Ragweed had a deal with Universal South, but they were a self-made band. Felker took note.

"They weren't Nirvana, and they weren't Garth Brooks, you know?" Felker says of Ragweed. "And I thought you had to be one of those two things to succeed as a musician at that point in time. Then, these guys showed up, and they sang cool rock and roll songs, but they played country songs too. They made it all seem very organic, like they were a garage band. It felt like they were just me and my buddies back home. And, they were from Oklahoma. They were from nowhere, and they actually saw real success. They were such a lighthouse for people like me that didn't think it was really possible to do anything with music other than go to Nashville and get a record deal."

Without Ragweed, there is every chance that there is no Turnpike. But without Turnpike, there's no Boys From Oklahoma. It's another in an endless series of full-circle moments to come from Stillwater's Red Dirt bars, campfires, and back porch picking sessions.

"Stillwater was *the* place in my mind," Felker says. "It was Nashville, to me, or L.A. I'm from a town of 700 people, so Stillwater was as big as it got in my mind. I felt like I had my fingers on the pulse of what music could be, and where I was supposed to be.

"I was in my early 20s when I got there, and I was working for Mercury Marine. Then, I started playing on The Strip at night. That was where I met Kyle. He'd been playing with Bo Phillips, and I think I maybe got some opening gigs.

"I got to meet Bo, Jason Eady, Johnny Burke, and Ryan Bingham at a fundraiser after Brandon Jenkins had all his shit stolen. I met all of them at the White Elephant down in Fort Worth. I actually had a show there. My buddy, Kyle Whitfield, pulled some strings when I had no business there whatsoever. But, I got to go, and I got to meet some people. The Dedringers were there. Stoney [LaRue] was there. I remember Bingham playing that 'Hard Times' song, right before he became, you know, the biggest thing in the world."

Felker had left Stillwater by the time he and RC Edwards formed Turnpike, but he carried with him a blueprint for succeeding as an independent band. He had also immersed himself in Red Dirt history and the likes of the late Bob Childers and Tom Skinner.

"Childers was still there," Felker recalls. "He was still hanging out when I lived there. He was friends with all my bluegrass buddies. I met Sam Parks there, and he plays in my bluegrass band now when he can. There was really a kickass bluegrass crowd when I was in Stillwater."

He keeps it under-the-radar, but Felker has made a habit of showing up at bluegrass festivals with Parks, Thomas Trapp, Tony Spatz, and a handful of others, like he did in fall 2024 at the Oklahoma International Bluegrass Festival, calling the group "Evan Felker and Friends."

"The bluegrass stuff I do now? That stems from being in Stillwater."

Felker recalls Stillwater as a melting pot. As much as anything, that's one avenue through which to understand the range in sounds that Red Dirt has, and how a band as country as Turnpike and as rock and roll as Ragweed can be considered part of the same genre of music.

Felker, Nix, and Edwards, along with guitarist Ryan Engleman, utility man Hank Early, and drummer Gabe Pearson — plus Bukka Allen sitting in on keys — treated The Boys From Oklahoma as the biggest shows of their careers. But when their sets finished and Ragweed took the stage, they reverted to fans. Nix returned during Ragweed's set each of the four nights to add fiddle to "On a Cloud" and perform it with Canada. Meanwhile, Felker added harmonica to Ragweed's "The Brooklyn Kid" on the opening night and sat in to sing the raucous third verse of "Carney Man" with Ragweed on the other three nights, not bothering to hide his grin in the process.

Felker knows there are parallels between Ragweed's return and Turnpike's, but he is quick to point out that each band means something different to Red Dirt and Oklahoma, largely because of how music has evolved over both groups' careers, and especially during Ragweed's 15 years off the road.

"Their story is very different than ours," Felker says. "They're almost mythical to us. To people who are my age and a little older who were there, they sort of sum up a generation. To see them get to come back like this, at some of the biggest shows in Oklahoma that have ever happened, it's fucking insane."

The Turnpike Troubadours on stage during a show in April 2024 in Baton Rouge, Louisiana.

THE TURNPIKE TROUBADOURS

NEVER SAY NEVER

The Price of Admission

If you want to call the Turnpike Troubadours the best band in America, you won't find me trying to stop you. But even if that bit is up for debate, this part is not: Turnpike walked out on stage the first night of The Boys From Oklahoma and dropped the best country album of this year or any other in recent memory.

The album in question is *The Price of Admission*, an 11-track record Turnpike released at 11 p.m. Oklahoma time on April 10 after a week of hints and easter eggs.

It started when the band released a song, "Be Here," exclusively to TouchTunes jukeboxes — a callback to Turnpike's 2023 album *A Cat in the Rain*, which was accidentally revealed early via a "leak" to TouchTunes. (What actually happened was the release date of the album's first single changed, and every digital music service except TouchTunes got the memo.) Then, a series of billboards advertising the album peppered the main roads into Stillwater.

It marks the sixth studio album for Turnpike and the second in a row produced by Shooter Jennings. With Red Dirt as a genre enjoying its greatest popularity — between Ragweed's reunion and a series of rising stars like Wyatt Flores, Kaitlin Butts and Josh Meloy drawing eye-popping crowds and streaming numbers — *The Price of Admission* serves as a reminder that Turnpike is still the genre's torchbearer and they will brook no passing on the left or the right.

The band is at its lyrical and musical peak across the board, and the record will surely rival their 2010 debut *Diamonds and Gasoline* as the best of the band's projects.

Unlike *A Cat in the Rain*, which was painstakingly crafted in the wake of Turnpike's self-imposed break from 2019-2022, *The Price of Admission* came together in a matter of weeks, in early 2025 at Sunset Sound Studio 3, which Jennings has the exclusive lease on in Los Angeles.

Felker wrote or co-wrote nine of the songs on the record. The two songs that came from someone other than him are "Ruby Ann," written by Lance Roark and Turnpike's bass player RC Edwards, and "Nothing You Can Do," written by Kyle Nix, who plays fiddle. In a significant departure from most of his songwriting catalog, however, Felker embraced co-writing for this project, collaborating with Nix and John Fullbright as well as Ketch Secor of Old Crow Medicine Show and Dave Simonett of Trampled by Turtles on four of the tunes. Fullbright's hometown of Okemah, Oklahoma, is Felker's adopted home. Secor and Simonett have both had their bands featured on bills opening for Turnpike in the past two years.

A few weeks before the concerts and album release, I spoke to both Evan Felker and Shooter Jennings about this project. Here's how they see it.

Evan Felker

First of all, it hasn't been all that long between albums by Turnpike standards. ***A Cat in the Rain*** **came out in 2023. So, what's behind this one, and how did it come about?**
We decided that we wanted to get back in the studio and just stay as active as we can. It's very easy for us to just start touring and not have plans for the studio, so we more or less just decided to do this one as soon as we could.

There's 11 songs on this album, and you wrote or co-wrote nine of them. What was your songwriting process like for this one?
It was not a long one, other than the first one ("On the Red River"). I wrote it with Ketch, and it took place over the longest period of time — maybe a couple of months. Then, the rest of them just sort of *happened*.

I sat down for 30 days and wrote. We got everything ready for the record, and then we finished them in the studio at the end of that 30 days.

Most of them, I wrote right here at home.

What was it like working with Shooter Jennings the second time around?

It was even more fun than the first time. We've gotten to be really good friends. He comes out on the road with us sometimes now, and he's like family to us.

It was a lot of fun, and it moved quickly, and we found that made it a very creative process from start to finish. We never got worn out or bogged down in things, and that's Shooter. He made it an extremely gratifying process the entire time.

Tell me about the collaborations with Ketch Secor and Dave Simonett.

We got to play some shows with Ketch, and Old Crow Medicine Show has been one of my favorite bands for a long time. The way those guys write, and the way they play, has had a huge impact on my songwriting. They helped me create a sort of framework for how I think a song comes together — or what's *good* about it when it comes together, at least.

Anyway, we played these shows and I just got hooked up with Ketch, and I was kind of going out on a limb with him. Because, what I like to do when I'm starting the writing process is, just set a day and *go*. Somebody get a project going! For this one, I was lucky enough to sit in a room with Ketch, and we took it back and holed up and wrote a really long, in-depth, overcooked narrative of a song.

Now, I met Dave through Steve Rinella, who does *MeatEater*. (Rinella is the host of the television show and podcast *MeatEater* as well as The History Channel's *Hunting History with Steven Rinella*.) We released the last record, and I went on his podcast. I got to go up there, and he was having his 50th birthday party. Well, Dave was there, and we got to bullshitting, and it turns out that we both bird hunt. And, we've also done some shows together. I've been a fan of Trampled by Turtles for a really long time, going all the way back to when we were playing Whiskey Jim's in Tahlequah, back when that was still even a bar. We talked about that and got to laughing about it, and we kind of got to be buddies.

He came out with me and we kind of stomped around in the Texas

Panhandle going after quail this year. We were holed up out in a little farmhouse out there, and he had this song he had sent me. So, we sort of peddled around with ideas, and he ... kind of let me finish it!

He's a great writer, and he's a really great singer. He writes fun melodies, and it was just neat to get to work with him and all these people who I really find inspiring.

I love asking for backstories, so I'll ask about a couple of songs. "Be Here" is the first one on my mind.
I had a really good time working on all these songs, because if I had an idea that gave me a *feeling*, then I would pursue it. This record was all about trying to find songs in a very different manner than me overthinking things or trying to let people know I can write some cool lines or that I know a big word or whatever. I was not trying to impress anyone. I was trying to feel something.

So, I was thinking about being in rehab. The song is really written from my perspective. As far as my songs go, it is the most autobiographical thing that maybe I've ever written.

But, I have also wanted to write a sea shanty. So, I was thinking about that part (a background chorus repeating lines like "I really don't need to be here") being, like, the voice in your head. Going through that process with the character in the song, to me, felt like going on a journey.

Holy shit, dude.
Yeah. It felt like it was worth pursuing, so I just did it.

Another one that stopped me on the first listen was "What Was Advertised."

It was very much a stream of consciousness to just sit down and write something. And, it ended up being vaguely about me — maybe being drunk back when I romanticized that kind of life. It was back when I wanted to be this barroom poet, you know? This shitfaced-all-the-time sort of crooner.

You and your band have both come really far since then, and I'm wondering if there's any hopes you have for this record, in that spirit?
What's so fucking cool about this is that we just decided to say, "Hell with it," and not try to sell this record. We're just gonna put out a record, and then I'm gonna go write more songs. I just want to make things and put them out with no lag and no bullshit in between, you know?

Fuck. That's what I'm doing here too.
I just want to let something natural happen now that's much more like back when we put out *Diamonds and Gasoline*, and we finished it and then we just gave it to our friends. That feels more like what we're doing now again.

But, it also feels like the world of music, or the business, has gravitated that way for a lot of people. Zach Bryan really does everything all his own way, and that has probably inspired a lot of people to do that kind of stuff.

You forget that, like, that was part of what made you interesting when you started out — how you *thought* you were perceived. It's later that you get reprogrammed to do things "correctly," and sometimes, it's just really not all that correct. Or it's just one definition of it.

Shooter Jennings

Can we talk about Turnpike's new album?
Dude. We finished that a month ago. We did it in a month, too. We turned around that record in one month. It's wild.

What stands out is that Evan was so happy. He was very happy through the whole process. I've become very good friends with them. Those guys are my brothers. I got to travel with them last summer, playing piano, and I got to see what a great place everybody was in, and it was wild to watch because they were just killing it at their shows. Everybody is in, like, this "peak performance" form, and it was awesome to get to be a spectator — who was also on stage.

Then, we get to the studio. It was right after the fires in L.A., but because of where the studio is at, we were fine. And I've been in Sunset Sound Studio 3 for a year now, working on records in the same place. Last time around (recording *A Cat in the Rain*), I kind of had my hand tied behind my back, because we were limited on gear and limited on microphones. We just kind of had to work with the best stuff we had. This time around, we had everything we needed. We had the space, and I've been working on the sound in there for a *long* time. They came in, and it was amazing.

Evan wrote some of the best songs that he's ever written, handsdown. He was so focused and had them crafted around his vision for them, and we ended up making their most country record ever. I feel that was because of the material and where everybody was at — they were all in great spirits. They all worked their asses off, working long hours in a short, two-week period. But, we got it done.

We hit all these beautiful songs, and then they put all these really thoughtful parts down on all of them. It was like seeing one of the greatest American rock and country bands in their top form, operating at their best efficiency. It was awesome, and it was really special.

What did you think when you heard "Be Here" after it was finished?
I think "Be Here" is one of the most beautiful songs ever, you know?

If all things were right, that song would win a Grammy, like for Song of the Year, because to me, it's that good. It's just beautiful, and I think it's probably one of the greatest songs about rehab that's ever been done.

Aside from the process, what was the studio environment like with those guys?
Well, the thing with them is, they have Evan and RC, but they also have Hank, Kyle and Ryan, and they are these three lead players. What I learned on the last record is that they like to carve out parts and then work around them together. They'll sit and talk through them. Hank will start with an idea, or Kyle will start with an idea — Kyle wrote the music for a few songs this time around, and we got to work around what he had done a lot.

Some of the songs were pretty fleshed out, but there were ones where they didn't really know what direction they wanted to go, and we got to experiment a little bit, and we had a little room to stretch and try the best things out. We took a lot of things into consideration on this record, but the most important thing to me was that the sound of the record stayed true to Turnpike's early material. We had that in mind with *Cat in the Rain*, too, but that was such a transitional record; it was such a moment in time. This time, they're back, and they're at the top of their game, and they are really appreciative of their fans, so being true to Turnpike was what was most important. This time around, we wanted to make sure the record felt like a Turnpike record through and through. We didn't veer too far from that.

The more the record went on, the more everybody started getting really excited about how *country* it was.

NEVER SAY NEVER

The Great Divide

In the planning of The Boys From Oklahoma concerts, Cody Canada can only recall one time he made a real, honest-to-goodness demand: "One of the nights, I want The Great Divide to go on before Turnpike. I want them to get to play to a full stadium, with all that energy, because of what they mean to this music."

Canada got his wish. In fact, each artist in the support slots — The Divide, Jason Boland and the Stragglers, and Stoney LaRue — would go on to play in the "direct to Turnpike" slot at least one of the four days. The Divide got the honor on the first night of the week, allowing Mike McClure, JJ Lester, Scotte Lester, Kelley Green, and Bryce Conway to play to what is almost certainly the largest crowd of their lives.

McClure, the frontman of The Divide, is not the least bit surprised to learn of Canada's request.

"It was an amazing chance, and I would understand if we weren't on the show at all, honestly," McClure says. "Whatever I have done for Cody, he has paid me back in spades."

That "whatever" is more load-bearing than McClure is letting on. The Great Divide is the band that drew Canada to Stillwater in the early 1990s. It was McClure who Canada lived with long enough to find a songwriting mentor at that same time. For a hot minute, The Great Divide even considered adding Canada as a fifth member. When they decided not to do it, Canada went back to his hometown of Yukon, Oklahoma and formed Cross Canadian Ragweed. Then, McClure and

THE GREAT DIVIDE

The Divide started telling every promoter and club owner they encountered to book Ragweed — if they weren't already having Ragweed on their bill as an opener themselves.

Once The Great Divide got big enough to put on their own festivals — Like The Great Divide's Independence Day Jam at City Limits in Stephenville, Texas, or College Days at The Tumbleweed in Stillwater — they turned them into day-long celebrations of Red Dirt, with Ragweed, Jason Boland, and Stoney LaRue always on the bills.

"Growing up, watching Willie Nelson and seeing The Family Jams and the Picnics, I just thought, 'How cool would that be?' Well, at the time, we had some national attention coming our way, and it was a great way to say, 'Oh! Check out these guys too! Here are some friends of ours you should hear,'" McClure recalls. "For a little while, we had a chance to do that. The Fourth of July in Stephenville was that way. I can remember Jason Boland's first time down to City Limits was at our festival. But, I can also remember people doing it for us. Gary P. Nunn – we couldn't have even gotten into City Limits in the first place without him going, 'If you don't book The Great Divide, I'm not gonna play there either.' Him doing something like that for us made it easy for us to say, 'OK, now it's our turn, and we're gonna pay it back.' Then I watched those guys do the same thing.

"It's just paying back what people have given to us."

Stillwater, particularly The Farm — a patch of land on the west side of town where a farmhouse once housed most of the Red Dirt Rangers and where Bob Childers lived, and where everyone in Red Dirt would gather to play songs around campfires through most of the 1980s and all of the 1990s — was also where McClure cut his teeth, musically.

"It made me want to become a better songwriter," McClure says of Stillwater. "I'd come out of listening to '80s rock, and I'd just started getting into better lyric writers. When I moved to Stillwater and started to hang around The Farm, it was just more lyric-focused. Then, I started getting into songwriters like Robert Earl Keen, and the Texas folks like Steve Earle and Guy Clark — that school.

"When I started going out to The Farm, it was the first place that I'd play my originals and someone would listen to them. And, they wouldn't say, like, 'Aw, that sucked!' but you could tell what songs were working and what songs weren't. And then, you could play your songs and stack them up against other well-written songs. That was the first time I had a chance to be around that."

McClure often cites an encounter with Clark in Fort Worth as the turning point for him as a songwriter. He got the opportunity to pass a guitar back and forth with Clark after a show one night, and Clark was not impressed with McClure's writing and did not hide it. The experience nearly brought McClure to tears and definitely sent him looking for an Irish exit, but the late songwriting icon sensed that, too. Clark pulled McClure aside and said, "You can write. You're just not showing your ass. When you start showing your ass, you're gonna be just fine."

McClure didn't just take those words to heart, he imparted them on Canada, Boland, and the growing crop of young songwriters living and playing in Stillwater when The Divide's career took off. One night in the mid-1990s, Canada — not yet 20 years old — played a new song at The Wormy Dog while McClure sat at the bar. When he finished, McClure stood up, gave Canada a thumbs down, and sat back down.

"I didn't know I was a mentor to anyone," McClure says now. "These were our friends. Our sense of humor has always been breaking each other's balls, and that doesn't always translate with everyone. I knew I was older, but they were just my friends. I didn't know I was a role model. I'd have been a better one if I did."

Like Clark with McClure, Canada responded by challenging himself as a songwriter, and within five years he would write "Alabama," "Constantly," "Pay," "On a Cloud," and around 50 other songs that would come to define Red Dirt music for generations to come.

When The Divide went through their own breakup in 2003 — one that would last until 2010 — Ragweed was waiting to assume their role as Red Dirt's torchbearers. McClure became Ragweed's primary producer.

"I thought they could really go anywhere they wanted to," McClure says of Ragweed. "I'd see them go out and hold their own playing with Dierks Bentley, bigger shows like that. There's just something about that band, and it's Cody's writing and it's the rumbling of all them coming together, and it's unique. I feel that in the Great Divide, too. I can play Great Divide songs with other people, but it's not the same. It's just not. It's just some sort of cool chemistry that happens with people sometimes."

THE GREAT DIVIDE

Having long since reconciled with his own band — and having earned a bevy of awards in Texas for The Great Divide's 2022 record, *Providence*, in the process — McClure both hopes and believes that Ragweed can experience the same sort of happiness in their reunion.

"It's amazing," he says. "I start crying when I think about it, because I know how much baggage that he carried around with him, or how much anger that he held inside that he didn't resolve. This is the resolution of that, and it's just, like, 'God, it's great!' That's what I want to see for all my friends, just some sort of deliverance like that. You tend to look back on the 10 percent that was bad and not the 90 percent that was an amazing, incredible journey. You make that 10 percent the whole hundred percent. I did that. Cody did that. I think a lot of people who leave bands do that. It just happens.

"To be able to reconcile that, and to think about how happy it's gonna make their fans, I just can't believe it, you know?"

The Great Divide make their Grand Ole Opry debut in July 2024.

THE GREAT DIVIDE

NEVER SAY NEVER

Jason Boland and The Stragglers

"It's got this real broad way of appealing, so that anybody can take it in," Jason Boland tells me. "The Red Dirt scene was so involved with the service of the song, and the sake of the song — to quote Townes Van Zandt — that it is mind-blowing how commercially successful it got."

In summing up how Red Dirt can be both very much a rock genre and very much a country genre — not to mention the elements of blues and folk that permeate the scene — Boland is speaking from his own lived experience. When he formed Jason Boland and The Stragglers circa 1998 in Stillwater, he put together the band that would set the bar for the country side of Red Dirt for more than a decade. Even if that torch was passed to one-time Stragglers openers the Turnpike Troubadours, Boland has never wavered from his hard-driving country sound.

So, perhaps no partnership underscores the range of Red Dirt than Cody Canada and Jason Boland. When you understand just how important Cody Canada and Cross Canadian Ragweed were to Boland during the earliest years of The Stragglers, you understand why the scene has the diverse sound it claims. No band opened more for Ragweed between 1998 and 2003 than The Stragglers, and no two artists played together in and around Stillwater more than Canada and Boland during that time. Red Dirt's newest country voice and its hardest rocker were the partnership that carried the genre into the 2000s.

Once Stoney LaRue joined that fray, bars in Tulsa, Stillwater, and Austin relished putting together three-show concerts featuring LaRue, the Stragglers, and Ragweed.

Now, they have returned home to play an absolutely astounding four-night run of shows at The Boys From Oklahoma. They're also going into the Oklahoma Music Hall of Fame together — along with LaRue and The Great Divide — formally inducted on Saturday during the third of the four shows.

"Like any musician that doesn't ever want to get hung up on the acclaim — because you can't convince a lot of people — for bands like us, that's not the reason we do it," Boland says. "It really is that weird service of the song. It's that addiction to creating a song that didn't exist before, and being proud of it. It's also playing a song that you wrote, that still moves you, and you're still communicating with it."

"A painting is up in a museum, and you can go look at it a million times. It's cool, but it will always be the exact same thing. An album is the same way. But, live music is something where you get to go watch this art happen again, and it will always be a little bit different."

Boland took the stage at The Boys From Oklahoma on the heels of a brand-new album, *The Last Kings of Babylon*, released the month before. The record is true to Boland's honky-tonk core, featuring a handful of songs poised to become classics in his catalog, like "The Next to Last Hank Williams" and his cover of Jimmy LaFave's "Buffalo Return to the Plains."

If he sounds fresh and recharged in his music on *The Last Kings of Babylon* — wry and defiant of the constraints, perceived or real, that he and his independent Red Dirt contemporaries have long felt — it may just be that country music is finally ready for Jason Boland. Nearly every force driving the current renaissance in new country music is one that Boland embodies so thoroughly that it cannot be construed as a buzzword:

Authentic? Boland has been writing his own music from the outset.

Traditional? Rarely has Boland recorded or toured without a steel guitar and fiddle. He mixes ballads with waltzes and hard-driving two-steppers and delivers them with a baritone voice that commands attention.

When these qualities were out of favor in country music for the first two decades of his career, Boland was unapologetic. Now that the artists like Zach Top and Braxton Keith have made those qualities all the rage, Boland seems made for the moment. When he sings "Every generation has it figured, then in the middle of the game, the rules have changed," on "The Next to Last Hank Williams," it's impossible to imagine Boland is referencing anyone other than himself.

"That song started out kind of talking about country music in an interconnected world where you may live out somewhere rural, but what does that really have to do with country?" Boland says of the song.

"We've heard what pop country's answer was to that. It was this cartoonish version with pickup trucks, beer, blue jeans, and dirt roads. Then, Americana split down this other way where you had a western shirt and bandana and double bass, and you were making cowboy music. Well, we've always just sat there asking, 'What's valid and cool in country music like it was when Dwight Yoakam and Steve Earle hit?' They were different artists, pushing country and folk music in interesting ways. Well, what do we have to say in that? 'Next to Last Hank Williams' started with that dichotomy, and then it just became a tune about independent artists who go out there and just *play*."

The juxtaposition of the brand new album and the trip through his extensive catalog during The Boys From Oklahoma will also serve as a testament to the songwriter in Boland. "The Next to Last Hank Williams" and "Pearl Snaps" were written 25 years apart, but they draw upon the same perspectives of a slightly-jaded crooner assessing the world he lives in and plays in.

"I think you're always looking," Boland says of songwriting. "Waiting *is* looking for songs. I don't like anything that's contrived. I'm always talking about the line you have to walk in folk or country. It's not rock and roll. It can be campy. It can be funny. It can be lighthearted and it can be tongue-in-cheek. But, for me, it really has to be balanced. I used to listen to a lot of Tom T. Hall, and that's stuff that doesn't have to be the most serious all the time — until, when it is serious, it is *very* serious. I just try to always take people on the ups and downs with me. If I go out and ever try to look for something clever, it wouldn't be honest, to me. So, I just let it happen, really."

It's a worldview he fine-tuned in Stillwater. His career would take him around the world — brushes with fame, more than one near-death experience, sobriety, and eventually settling into a role as a veteran of Red Dirt capable of sustaining an independent career indefinitely — but it is forever rooted in the artists he shares the bill with at The Boys From Oklahoma.

There is one, in particular, though, that he's especially looking forward to seeing play.

"I'm so excited just to see Ragweed do it again. Bands like Great Divide and Ragweed were very special to me. They were inspirational. It was just amazing to watch people play their music the way they wanted to hear it, and stick to their guns about it, too. Even when The Divide or Ragweed had some more label-type folks behind them, they were so fiercely defensive of their process and how the music was produced.

"Over anything else, I'm just excited to see Ragweed playing again. And then, have everybody remember, when we're talking about how far this all has come, just how important they were to it. They were a cultural phenomenon, and it was awe-inspiring to be around it. I'm thankful to still be hanging out with them, and just excited to see it all happen."

Jason Boland and the Stragglers play at the 2024 Jackalope Jamboree in Pendleton, Oregon.

JASON BOLAND AND THE STRAGGLERS

NEVER SAY NEVER

Stoney LaRue

"Red Dirt was something that the world needed at the time," Stoney LaRue says, recalling the music options available to Oklahomans in his formative years.

"You're talking about the heartland of America. At the time, there was just country or just rock and roll. There was 100.5, the KATT, in Oklahoma City, or there was whatever country station there was, and we were all glued to them. Well, now, there's not only streaming services, and there's not only outer space music, but there's also a genre for Red Dirt music. a

"It's not only in the state of Oklahoma anymore. It's worldwide. That's given us quite a platform to go out and be recognized on, and as a result, there are people who have gone and taken it farther than we even have."

That's a strong statement coming from LaRue, a Stillwater native whose musical awakening came while living in The Yellow House with Cody Canada and Jason Boland — literally, a yellow house just off of the Oklahoma State University campus that succeeded The Farm as ground zero for Red Dirt Music scene in the late 1990s — and playing acoustic shows nearly every night at The Wormy Dog Saloon, Willie's Saloon, Eskimo Joe's, or any fraternity party that would have him.

He befriended Red Dirt legends like Bob Childers and Randy Crouch, both of whom LaRue has covered in his nearly 30-year career. He co-wrote with Brandon Jenkins, and during The Boys From Oklahoma concerts, he played a pair of Jenkins tunes: "Feet Don't Touch The Ground" and "Down in Flames."

LaRue now lives in Texas on a lake in suburban Dallas, and he tours relentlessly, but he still feels tied to Stillwater and his Red Dirt upbringing no matter where he's playing.

"It seems like yesterday, still," LaRue tells me. "I remember you coming over. I remember looking out the window whenever I finally got a room there [in The Yellow House], and watching Boland and the Stragglers pull out in their Suburban with their trailer and thinking, 'I can't wait to do that, instead of just playing in this one-horse town.'

"I came into this scene as kind of a top-40 guy, trying to emulate other artists and do a bunch of covers and stuff. I never thought about writing until I got around Boland and Cody and [Mike] McClure. It's kismet, or something.

"Those songs raised me, not figuratively but literally. So, it's like sharing your family with the world, you know?"

Some time around late 2001 or early 2002, The Yellow House fell out of the hands of the artists who lived there. Boland moved to Texas, as The Stragglers had gained a stronghold in the Lone Star State. Canada and Ragweed had already made the move by then. LaRue, then, went full-bore into his own career. The first thing he did was join up with The Organic Boogie Band — which consisted of most of the iconic early Red Dirt band, Medicine Show — and release *Downtown*, an album the group recorded at Cain's Ballroom in Tulsa. With LaRue singing lead and the swampy, bluesy melodies of The Organic Boogie Band, he turned heads throughout Red Dirt and Texas music.

To follow that, LaRue formed his own band and called the group "The Arsenals," and they recorded The Red Dirt Album — with Mike McClure producing — which included a co-write with Bob Childers in "One Chord Song," as well as "Texas Moon" and a reprise of his autobiographical "Downtown."

But it was LaRue's next record that set up all that followed in his career. His *Live at Billy Bob's* record was recorded in 2006 and released in 2007. One of the songs on the record was a cover of Mike Hosty's "Oklahoma Breakdown," a bluesy-folk party tune in which the narrator takes his girlfriend "down to the river in the back of Fred's truck" for a night of debauchery despite her daddy's disapproval. The song showcased LaRue's vocal range, which may go down as the strongest in Red Dirt history, and it caught fire in Texas. In 2007, LaRue's cover of "Oklahoma Breakdown" became the best-selling single in all of Texas music. He emerged as a confident headlining artist and has remained one since. At the same time, he is one of the most-determined artists in Red Dirt to pay homage to Childers, Crouch, and the genre's forefathers who he considered mentors and friends.

So, what has changed for him, musically, in the two decades since he left that family?

"The names, probably, are what's most different," he says. "I was really guarded and jaded, without knowing what the word 'jaded' meant back then. 'I only like this music, and everything else sucks.' Whereas, now, 'Messy' is my new favorite song — by Lola Young. My mind has just grown, and it's because I got to have all these experiences."

LaRue also recognizes his days of running around with Canada and Boland are a thing of the past, but he appreciates The Boys From Oklahoma as much for the opportunity to play to top-tier crowds as for the chance to reconnect with the people who showed him the way back in his Yellow House days.

"I named my son C.J. after Cody Canada and Jason Boland," he says. "We aren't the same people that we were. We don't get the same experiences that we had. We go to our respective buses, and then we're out shooting across the highway to the next town, however many miles that may be away, to go do our own thing. But, it's like an 'atta boy' to each other, each time we see each other. We just pick up where we left off. There's no goodbye, there's just hiccups and hellos."

STONEY LARUE

NEVER SAY NEVER

Cody Canada and Stoney LaRue play at the 2024 Mile 0 Fest in Key West.

STONEY LARUE

NEVER SAY NEVER

Oklahoma Breakdown: The Mike Hosty Story

Mike Hosty spent the six months leading up to The Boys From Oklahoma shows bragging to his barroom crowds about having the most expensive song of the weekend. He didn't call it a "million-dollar song" or something simple like that. He did the math, factored in the length of the song and the attendance plus average ticket price before landing on a six-figure number and change as the value of "Oklahoma Breakdown."

"Oklahoma Breakdown" is the rare song — at least in the pre-Wyatt Flores era circa 2023 — to come out of Red Dirt circles that can be called a true hit. This first came courtesy of Stoney LaRue, who started covering Hosty's swampy, take-your-love-down-to-the-river tune at his live shows around the turn of the century before it found a spot on LaRue's 2005 *Live at Billy Bob's Texas* album. It would go on to become the best-selling single in Texas music for all of 2007.

But "Oklahoma Breakdown" had a second rise, too. The late Toby Keith included the song on his *Peso in My Pocket* album, and in 2022, it became the final single (not counting re-releases) in the career of the country music legend and Oklahoma native.

Hosty himself isn't Red Dirt, no matter how much the genre may want to claim him. Red Dirt claiming Mike Hosty would be like you or me laying claim to the sun because it happens to shine on us. He's a multifaceted musician, instrumentalist and songwriter — neither country, rock nor blues enough to be classified — who has made a life out of playing central Oklahoma bars like The Deli in Norman and JJ's Alley in Oklahoma City's Bricktown district. In three-plus decades, he's had brushes with massive, worldwide fame. It never quite stuck to him the way fans who turn out to hear his songs, and the Will Rogers-esque stories behind them, at his live shows most nights a week did. He has, at various times, been billed as part of the Sugar Free All-Stars, The Mike Hosty Trio, and The Hosty Duo, before he settled into his current one-man show that usually involves him playing a drum kit, an electric guitar, and a kazoo.

He's the sort of artist who leaves an impression, too. A core component of my own friendship with Chad Gamble — who you likely know as the drummer in Jason Isbell and The 400 Unit — is a memory of Hosty opening for Chad and his brother, Al, when the two played in The Gamble Brothers Band in the early 2000s. If Chad or I are in a social gathering today, the over-under on one of us bringing up Hosty's ode to severe weather, "Fraidy Hole," is five minutes.

But this isn't a chapter about Mike Hosty.

This is a chapter about a *documentary* about Mike Hosty.

I have shouted from the rooftops that my goal in my writing is to go beyond telling you that Red Dirt exists. I'm doing this because I want you to do what I have done for 25 years: Put your ear to the engine of Red Dirt and listen to it whirr. Do that, and you'll hear the people who have been trying to tell the world about this genre for half a century. I know this first-hand, because I was one of those people before a 2020 phone call from Evan Felker in which he told me, paraphrasing, "I'm sober. I'm happy. I plan on making music with Turnpike again, and it's ok to print it," became the first story I ever had blow up in *Rolling Stone* and enabled literally everything I've done as a music journalist since.

So when I see that it has been three years since *Oklahoma Breakdown: The Mike Hosty Story* was first released, and I think about the fact most people, even fans of Hosty, don't realize it's out there, I feel like it's a crime against Red Dirt. The documentary is a labor of love by director Christopher Fitzpatrick, who became enamored with Hosty's live shows back when Fitzpatrick was a student at The University of Oklahoma. Starting in 2016, he sat out to tell Hosty's story with a self-funded documentary he produced and directed that completely threads Hosty through Red Dirt. LaRue, Cody Canada, and Jason Boland all contribute — as does Red Dirt oracle and frequent "source close to the scene" in my books, Ragan Parkerson.

Oklahoma Breakdown is a documentary you need to see, whether you're a lifer in the genre or just feeling nostalgic because of Ragweed. I'll link to it — right here in the digital versions and in the appendix in print — and hope that helps. But I also think you should hear from the director himself, since we're here.

The rest of this chapter is a Christopher Fitzpatrick chapter. But it's a Mike Hosty chapter, too. See how that works? Here's me and Fitzpatrick having a back-and-forth in late 2024.

Bio question: Who are you, what were your college-era musical influences/tastes, and why did you end up at OU in the late 1990s?
I became an Okie when I was almost 3 — the first memory of my life was arriving to our new house in OKC — and lived there till the age of 10. I left kicking and screaming because all my friends were in OKC and my brother and I had become diehard Sooner fans. My high school musical influences were classic rock (Doors, Zeppelin superfan, Hendrix... etc). I liked pretty much everything you'd get on classic rock radio. That carried heavily over to my college days. I was defiant about Nirvana and preferred Pearl Jam, though the Smashing Pumpkins' first three albums took over as my favorites of the day. I didn't like 80-90 percent of the modern rock hits you'd hear on the legendary KDGE in DFW. I look back with regret of that time that I didn't dive deeper into Radiohead — now my favorite lifelong band, or at least go *see* Nirvana when I had the chance. Country was never really in the conversation for me in college, save for slight crossover bands like [Cross Canadian Ragweed], The Grateful Dead and the Allman Brothers. To me that was a cool way of listening to country songs. "Local" bands weren't something I knew much about — that changed with the Mike Hosty Trio. Nothing ever had hit me over the head like that. And they were, for the most part, accessible.

The answer to the last part really comes back to the beginning. I never got Oklahoma out of me (and still haven't). I was the kid who took sports abuse from Longhorn fans at the lunch table in middle school. I still maintained that state pride after moving, as a young teenager might. Even though I've lived most of my life in Texas, I have always considered myself an Okie at heart. I chased my older brother to OU to pursue similar interests — sports broadcasting.

What do you recall about Hosty playing in those days? What were your impressions of him then?
The first time I laid ears on the talents of Mike Hosty was at a fraternity party in the front lawn of the Kappa Sigma house at OU, in September 1995. The band Leghead was a late cancellation and we had an incredible amount of beer brought over by the Delta Upsilon house. They literally dumped like 30 cases on our front lawn. The party was legendary enough to get our chapter in hot water and on probation from further such functions. I don't know if we got in trouble for a noise violation, because Heater was really loud, and the guitar of Mike Hosty was cranked all the way up. I don't remember much else about that day other than my best friend got an MIP (Minor in Possession) and several members of the FIGI (Phi Gamma Delta) house across the street ate mushrooms and watched the whole damn thing from their roof. I thought, "Ok wow, there's some sort of cred points for that as a hometown band!"

A couple years later when I was of legal drinking age, a group of us piled in a car and headed toward a tiny dive bar in Norman called The Deli to see that guitar player who now had his own band, The Mike Hosty Trio. There was a line out the door, and the cover was $5. I don't know how that place didn't violate fire code but we somehow got in. When the band took stage, there were only three of them, fronted by that same face with a goatee and a ponytail. The downbeat started and the sound of blues and funk settled us in. When they eased to a crescendo it sounded like 10 people were on stage. They had this massive instrument that you might see on Sundays in church. Their sound fit right in with what I listened to in that time period. I don't remember if I loved Booker T and the MG's before Hosty, and I didn't understand at the time that the two bands used the same instrument (B-3 Organ) but as I think about it, that had a big effect on my music tastes going forward.

I would gravitate to The Meters a few years later. And I can trace it, from my experience, all back to those many nights out at The Deli watching The Hosty Trio. We'd go two times a month. It was perfect for the time, and I can 100 percent tie any confidence in getting on a dance floor with (or in the vicinity of) girls back to those Hosty shows. They were all feeling that irresistible Hosty groove too. The songs were VERY catchy with great harmonies, and there was nothing else like them around. No doubt the vibe in the place was full of positivity. You couldn't go to a Hosty show and NOT feel good. That remains today. Jokes (Hosty was still honing his craft at that) and smiles were abound. But the one thing that still makes my bones chill with fondness were those tasteful blues guitar licks that didn't try too hard and filled up the room with a tone that's unmistakable to this day. It's no surprise they cranked out five albums in five years, because they were in a creative apex — their musical prime.

What were your impressions of the Central Oklahoma music scene?
As mentioned in question one, I did not know much about anything "local" until Hosty. Now, everyone knew about The Chainsaw Kittens and The Flaming Lips. But beyond that, Wakeland was a band that had a big following (I never gave them much thought) and of course the Nixons with their hit "Sister". That was Norman/OKC music in my bubble. Once I got introduced to Hosty and the Deli scene, I got wind of similar bands like Jimijank and a band from Tulsa, The Jacob Fred Jazz Odyssey. The local scene seemed to appeal to fraternity kids who smoked a lot of pot. I'm so glad we at least had *something* because rock music was becoming a cesspool of: 1. bands trying to imitate Nirvana 2. record labels making decisions to save their asses from going under (i.e. signing bands that tried to imitate Nirvana).

It was a bad time for rock and roll. But I don't recall ever seeing a band that identified as country back in the late 90's, and if the Stillwater scene that was developing then came through Norman, I had no idea.

In the time between college and making this doc, did you stay abreast of Hosty's music and career?
Right about the time I graduated (fall 1998), I finally made it into The Deli for something I had seen advertised in a bathroom stall for several months. "Mike Hosty, solo, Sunday night". So maybe around finals week my final semester I had free time to drink on a Sunday night. I'd never really seen anyone play guitar and drums at the same time. So to

see this dude wearing a harp round his neck, with a 3-piece drum set-up at his feet, and play the same level of guitar I'd heard for the last 2-3 years on that same stage blew my damn mind. At some point into the set he ripped into an old Blind Willie Johnson number (most famously covered by Led Zeppelin), "In My Time of Dying". While he didn't play the whole 11-minute version I was familiar with, the indelible images I still carry with me today floored me. I knew at that moment that I'd be following this guy for the rest of my life or his — whichever ended first.

After then, I'd moved to Dallas-Fort Worth and would often come up to Oklahoma for work or to see family. If I had a night free, without fail, I was looking up live events in the area to see where Hosty, by then playing as The Hosty Duo, would be playing. I had no shame in going by myself but if I had co-workers in tow I would no doubt measure their enthusiasm as the night went on. I can count on one finger how many people (out of over hundreds by now) I've introduced to Hosty that didn't immediately come away as a fan.

What made you decide to turn it into a documentary?
I stumbled into the Mercury Lounge in Tulsa one night in 2016 to see a show entitled "Mike Hosty" on the bill. It was a Saturday, and he didn't have his longtime drummer, Mike Byars, with him. This was never the case on a weekend gig. And by this point he was on a level nobody could touch as a solo act. High level comedy, untouchable musicianship, perfect guitar tone and improv skills you just shake your head at. After many drinks, I came up to him after the show.

Me: "Hey, where's Byars?"

Hosty: "I'm by myself now."

Me: "For good?"

Hosty: "Yep."

I knew he had a major health scare a couple of years before this, and I'd always wanted to do *something* to explore his life in music. I had just become a freelance videographer about two months prior to this night. At this point in my career, I felt I had enough storytelling chops to make some sort of short documentary on the guy, providing nobody else was doing this already.

So I finally countered with: "Hey, I'd like to do a documentary about you. Would you be interested in something like that?"

Hosty: "Sure."

I don't think he thought anything of it and had no idea what it'd turn into. People in my field say this kind of thing all of the time. "I'd like to do a documentary on X". People *not* in the film world say something like, "Man, that would make a cool documentary" about one hundred times a minute. And, no doubt, he'd heard similar comments from people that dabbled in the film world. But, this is something I'd stewed on long enough and the timing was right in my life and in his. So after getting barely enough gear (a camera, tripod, and enough lights and limited audio gear), I showed up at a gig on November 30th, 2016, at Dan's Silverleaf in Denton, Texas and just started recording his show. A week later I drove up to his house in Norman for an interview, and we were off.

In making it, what struck you about Hosty the most?
In a way, he was always a musical icon of mine. And I've always admired how accessible and kind he is to his fans. He's been known to finish a gig, then see people show up after getting off their night shift, and go back on stage and play whatever song they request. He actually did this for me, once. That is not normal. But as connected as he is with the audience when he's on the stage, he was pretty guarded about his personal life. This took me a while to understand why. He really values his family time, which is a big reason he isn't a massive rock star. I'm not alone in saying that he could have been world famous if he really wanted to. I don't know any musician/entertainer who can do what he does on a stage. Yet here he is, charging $5 covers at mostly shitty dive bars across Oklahoma, and loving every minute of it. Then he would get to come home to his wife and kid after most shows. Very few working musicians have that kind of lifestyle.

Last question. In making it, what struck you about Hosty's relationship to Red Dirt music, and the larger Texas and Americana scenes, since he's decidedly none of those?
Before interviewing Hosty that first time at his house, I was Red Dirt ignorant. I'd never associated Hosty with country music because the majority of his incredible guitar tone is rooted in the blues and blues rock. Obviously I knew the name Stoney LaRue because of his ties to "Oklahoma Breakdown," but I didn't have a real idea of how big of a hit that was. I had definitely heard of Cross Canadian Ragweed and at some point ended up in a guitar circle strumming along to

OKLAHOMA BREAKDOWN

"Boys from Oklahoma." But when Hosty shyly suggested I might interview Cody Canada for the project, I didn't know who that was. When Cody said yes without hesitation, I had a good feeling about where this was headed. Hearing what Cody, Stoney, and Jason Boland had to say about Hosty was pretty eye-opening, but the biggest landmark moment was filming at the Larry Joe Taylor Festival in Stephenville in 2017. I interviewed Boland right before he walked out to a Friday, late afternoon, liquored-up crowd. Stoney was the closer. It was a scene I never knew existed on this level. In the documentary you see Stoney's version of "Oklahoma Breakdown" from behind the stage, as a sea of people (30,000+) sing every word — it still gives me chills thinking about it. That's the moment I knew how important Hosty was to Red Dirt and that I had something bigger in this documentary than I ever imagined. In the late '90s, these guys were young kids when the Mike Hosty Trio played The Wormy Dog on Penny Beer Night. They were admittedly in awe and, even Cody Canada admits, intimidated. They looked up to him then, and now as big stars in their field, have nothing but glowing things to say about him, because as they say, "Gotta keep spreadin' the Dirt".

As far as the larger Texas and Ameriana scenes, you don't hear much about him and he's just not represented by those groups like he is Red Dirt. But anyone in those scenes that have ever laid eyes on a Mike Hosty live show doesn't forget about him. He's like this little secret that's been passed around the region, and now these Nashville session and hired tour guns get to have their fun with ultra-inside baseball music knowledge of one of the greatest musicians nobody knows about. Guys in Jack White and Jason Isbell's bands are playing Hosty tunes on their tour bus. From what I know, the Turnpike guys go way back with Hosty and I bet not one of them has a bad word to say about the guy. *They* look up to *him*. And I can only imagine the heavy hitters he'd be on stage with nightly if he only wanted to. The line would form to the left. But that's not who he is.

NEVER SAY NEVER

I Am Trying to Break Your Heart

I do not know how many Josh Crutchmer books you have read, but, personally, I have read several. One thing I can tell you about a Josh Crutchmer book is, it's gonna have some allegory.

So if you are wondering if Chapter 10 of a book about Cross Canadian Ragweed reuniting on the campus of Oklahoma State University just might be about "On a Cloud," I am here to tell you that, yes, Chapter 10 is about "On a Cloud."

You will get to the proper concert chapters in due course, but there was one moment during each show that passed unchanged from night-to-night.

Each time, roughly 90 minutes into the set, Jeremy Plato, Grady Cross, and Randy Ragsdale left the stage. Cody Canada remained in the spotlight, guitar in hand, and Turnpike Troubadours fiddle player Kyle Nix stepped in alongside Canada. As a montage of friends, family, and musical icons who had passed on played on the video board behind them, Canada and Nix performed the ballad from Ragweed's 2003 self-titled "Purple" album, written from the perspective of someone whose time on Earth has ended., The song implores grieving loved ones, "Look toward the heavens when I cross your mind, and you just might see my face on a cloud."

Each night, most fans in the crowd responded to the song by turning on their phone lights and holding them up, creating a backdrop of what looked like thousands of stars inside an otherwise intentionally darkened Boone Pickens Stadium.

Each night, before this scene played out, I stepped to the microphone, at Canada's request, and told more than 45,000 people what "On a Cloud" was about. When I finished, I asked Andrea Hancock, my friend and this book's editor, to join me.

I did it because I wanted the stadium to see Andrea, known to family as Andie, and clap for her more than I wanted them to clap for me. I did it because that moment summed up just how deep and tangled Red Dirt's roots run — for Stillwater, for OSU, for the artists who make up the scene, and for myself.

I did it, and I am writing this right now, because I am trying to break your heart.

The song was written mere days after the January 2001 plane crash that killed 10 members of the OSU basketball family returning from a game at Colorado University, hence its placement as the tenth chapter in this book. I know this because I was in Cody Canada's living room the day after he wrote it, listening to him play it for me, and bawling my eyes out. I was the sports editor of *The Daily O'Collegian*, the campus newspaper at Oklahoma State University. My main job was covering the Cowboy basketball program, but on January 27, I was not covering the game. I was at the Wormy Dog Saloon in Stillwater, watching Cross Canadian Ragweed throw a release party for their *Highway 377* album. After that night, I went back to my job. That means, at age 22, I had to direct the most intimate, important coverage of this tragedy for the same campus and community of which I was a part.

That's enough background to understand how my own ties that bind me to Red Dirt are threaded with the heartbreak of that night.

In the nearly quarter-century that has passed since, Canada and I have told that story to crowds around the world to introduce "On a Cloud." Sometimes — such as at Ragweed's no-longer final show at Joe's On Weed Street in Chicago in 2010 — the introduction itself became a poignant, heavy part of the concert.

By the time Cody Canada and The Departed landed their annual Joe State Tailgate shows at Eskimo Joe's the night before OSU's homecoming football game each fall, the introduction to "On a Cloud" had become essential to the song. The lyrics and the story worked together to convey the gravity of its origins, and it resonated deeply with the fans gathered at OSU.

In 2022, I introduced the song, and then I asked Andie — who was an infant when her father, Will Hancock, was one of the 10 lost in the crash — to join me on stage as I talked about it. The adopted memorial phrase for the tragedy is "Remember The Ten." I'd been feeling for a while that I should be wearing that on my sleeve when I had the chance, and it felt right that night. I made a speech, Andie at my side, and we waved and walked off when Cody started playing. Before the last verse, though, Shannon Canada brought Andie and me — along with my wife, also named Andrea — back on stage. We locked arms and swayed behind Cody as he finished the song. It was emotional, but the emotions were comfort and community. It was a moment.

Andie and I repeated the moment at the Joe State tailgate the night before Oklahoma State's 2024 homecoming game. Only this time, all of Ragweed was present. This was the weekend that cemented the reunion. Grady Cross and Randy Ragsdale — and their families — took the evening in from a VIP tent at the side of the stage. At the end of the night, Cody asked if we would do the same thing at the reunion shows. I texted Andie, and she replied, "Fastest yes I ever typed."

That's how she and I ended up on stage introducing "On a Cloud" at Boys From Oklahoma. I scripted what I'd say, so as to keep it short and on point, and for the most part, the moment played out very similarly each night. The only deviation came on the second night, when my cousin, Wes Crutchmer, wore Nate Fleming's 2000-01 OSU basketball jersey to the concert. Wes and the Fleming family are friends, and he thought it would be a nice touch to honor Nate — another one of the 10 lost in the crash — that night. So Wes stepped on stage and allowed the crowd to see him in Fleming's jersey.

But the how is the easy part of this story. My struggle was with *what* I'd say. It's one thing to tell this story to a bar or a block party. It's another to do it four nights in a row, to a crowd totalling upwards of 180,000 people, including many who lost family members or very close loved ones. If I picked too much at my own scars, I'd take the focus off of them. But if I glossed over it and, say, didn't talk about exactly where and how we experienced the tragedy, then it's pointless. "On a Cloud" has since gone on to be so much bigger than that night. It has comforted thousands, if not hundreds of thousands, of people in their times of loss. The right thing to do, if any of those people were present at the concerts, was to show them where it came from and just how intertwined it is with one of the darkest days in Stillwater history.

The only way I knew to make that point was to stand in front of everybody in the stadium and relive my own pain for 90 seconds. Let folks feel a bit of the moment that song came from. Beforehand, I told my friends, "When I talk about 'Cloud' out there, I am trying to break your heart." Once I realized that Andie and I had to go out there and bring the party down, there was no reason to half-ass it.

That's what went through my mind when I wrote the "On a Cloud" introduction in an orange-leather journal that had been gifted to me by Dr. Kayse Shrum when I gave OSU's fall commencement address in December 2024.

This is what I wrote, and this is what I said.

On a Cloud Intro

For 25 years, I have watched Red Dirt serve as a comfort to Stillwater, to OSU, and to our wider music family in times of tragedy. When we lost Red Dirt icons like Bob Childers, Tom Skinner, and Brandon Jenkins, when we lost family like Johnny C., Mandi and JC Ragsdale, and when we lost friends, or pets, or even livelihoods, this scene always rallied. A near-constant presence in that comfort has been Cross Canadian Ragweed — in spirit, in person, or in song.

I saw this first-hand on January 27, 2001, when I was the sports editor of the *O'Collegian* newspaper here on campus, and I chose not to travel to cover the Cowboys' basketball game at Colorado because I wanted to go down the street to the old Wormy Dog, and watch Ragweed release their *Highway 377* record, and we watched as the bar TVs relayed one of the most heartbreaking nights in our community's history, with the loss of 10 members of Cowboy basketball that day, and we cried together. Then, through the sorrow, Ragweed played for us that night until they turned out the lights.

Five days later, I witnessed how that music can heal, when I sat in Cody's living room and watched him play a song he wrote the night before called "On a Cloud" for the first time.

24 years after that I'm here as evidence of that healing. That experience is what motivates me to write about Red Dirt and share it in Rolling Stone, and in the books I write. With me tonight is Andrea Hancock. She was two months old that night in January 2001, and she

lost her father. Today, along with her family, she is the embodiment of what it means to Remember the Ten. She is also the editor of those books I write, and she is my friend.

I hope we feel that spirit again tonight, soon after another tragedy in Stillwater. I hope, when you hear this song, you find a hint of peace or comfort. Because, as Cody said in February 2001, the first time he sang "On a Cloud" at the Wormy Dog — That's the Stillwater we know.

I AM TRYING TO BREAK YOUR HEART

The introduction to "On a Cloud" on Sunday, April 13, 2025. (Jimmy Flex)

The introduction to "On a Cloud" on Thursday, April 10, 2025. (Clay Billman)

I AM TRYING TO BREAK YOUR HEART

NEVER SAY NEVER

Grady Cross

It takes exactly one question for Grady Cross to be hit with a wave of emotion.

"Man, a lot is going through my head," Cross says. We have stolen ourselves a spot out of view at Dante's in Key West, Florida, where The Smokin' Oaks are about to play a mid-day pool party at the 2025 Mile 0 Fest. The weather is uncooperative, as a cold front that brought snow to the Gulf Coast in the northern part of the state has brought a brisk, 40-mile-per-hour north wind to this island. It's throwing Cross for a loop as he works with his son, Slaid, to set up the Oaks' set. When I ask him about the prospect of playing with Ragweed again, it hits him like a ton of bricks, and he stops to compose himself before finishing his thought.

"Number one, I am glad to be talking to my friends again. Whether we played music or not, that has to come first, and that's where we started back up. Next is my family. Putting these shows together in Stillwater, that's huge, to me, and it's unreal. It's a big damn deal, you know?"

Cross's relationship with Cody Canada and Randy Ragsdale dates back to elementary school in Yukon, Oklahoma. When they formed Ragweed back when the entire group was still in high school, his goals were pretty simple: Practice and play. They did the first at Ragsdale's house, with the blessing of Randy's father, the late Johnny C. Ragsdale. But the first time someone took notice of what those kids were doing, it hooked Cross for life.

GRADY CROSS

"When we started this band, it was in Randy's living room — Johnny's. We got to the point where we were doing eight-hour practices every day, trying to get tighter and better. That was it. We just wanted to play music — to go out and *play*. Don't get me wrong, we had plenty of times where nobody showed up, but when you have those nights where the whole crowd shows up, it really bites you, and you know it's forever.

"For something inside you, it *feels like* forever."

When Ragweed caught fire, especially in the early years of their Universal South deal and the run of three albums — *The Purple Album* (2002), *Soul Gravy* (2004), and *Garage* (2005) — that took the band from a regional hit to one that could sell out theaters from coast to coast, Cross allowed himself to get caught up in the moment and the personal relationships that Ragweed forged with their fan base.

"God, it felt so unreal," he recalls. "Watching the crowds get bigger. Watching the album sales and getting played on radio, it was fast. We played a ton, and, honestly, we fed off the people watching us. We developed friendships with the fans, with the promoters. We developed this loyalty with the people who came out for us. We'd go on cruise ships with them. It's pretty amazing to play music for a living and watch people smile back at you and sing you songs back."

He also understands that there's a dynamic that exists within the four members of Ragweed that makes their shows unique — some unexplainable combination of energy and camaraderie that only shines through with this combination of musicians.

"There's no better feeling in the world," he says of playing with Ragweed. "It's like this for anybody who plays rhythm, but when you get locked in, it's like a machine. I try to lock in on the snare. And I can tell when Randy's on, and Jeremy's locked in, and Cody is locked in to *everybody*, it just works well. I enjoy playing rhythm guitar. I like sitting back and getting in a groove with the boys."

Ragweed's 2010 breakup was intense. The three peaks of Red Dirt music, pre-2022, were followed by band splits that corresponded in pain and heartache to the heights of the peaks. The Great Divide's breakup in 2003 took eight years to patch up. The Turnpike Troubadours' 2019 hiatus was never intended to be final, although Evan Felker said in hindsight that he was "done with music" in its immediate wake. That one lasted three years. But Ragweed's was the hardest one to unravel. When it happened, though, Cross tried to make the most of it.

"I bought a bar in Yukon, Oklahoma," he says. "This was the old 50-Yard Line. That's actually where Cross Canadian Ragweed got its start. Of course, we've done remodeling. I changed the name. I bought it 15 years ago. It's Grady's 66 Pub. We have live music every weekend. It's still going. I have a record store next to it — Grady's Green Room music shop. We sell records and strings and some of the stuff you might need."

Five years into his post-Ragweed life, Cross made another change, swearing off alcohol for good.

"Number one, I did it for my family," Cross says of his wife, Robin, and his children, Slaid and Charlie. "I had a lot of fun, but I had to make a decision for my health and my family. And, it's the best decision I've ever made in my life. I'm happy to be here, to be honest with you, and happy to have a good family."

Music remained a mainstay in the family.

Grady's 66 Pub quickly became a regular bar stop in metro Oklahoma City for artists in Red Dirt, Texas, and Americana circles. But it was Slaid's interest in music that really drew Cross's time and attention over the past 15 years.

"I'm sitting here in Key West, and everything is full-circle. It has come full-circle," he recalls. "What I mean by that is, I feel like maybe our kids kind of helped bring us back — or had something to do with it. It's full-circle. What's a trip is watching Dierks and Willy (Canada) up there jamming, and watching Slaid play, and they're playing some of the same stages we played. We went to the Blue Light in Lubbock, and Slaid is up there playing some of my same gear, same guitar, same stage, and covering a song that maybe we used to cover. That's a trip. That's full circle."

By the time he shared this reflection, Ragweed's reunion was sealed. Six months earlier, he never could have envisioned such a conversation. The invitation to play again came from Jon Folk. It happened quickly.

Cross recalls: "I kind of missed the email at first. But, Randy had texted me and said, 'Hey dude. What's up?' And I go, 'What's going on?'

Because I *know* that he wants something.

"Well, he goes, 'Jon Folk's gonna call you. He wants to sit down and have dinner with us in Oklahoma City.' And Randy is like, 'It's *good*, dude.' So, (Cross' wife) Robin and I went down and had dinner with Jon and Ragweed's accountant, and he listened to us, and it wasn't really that hard. We were in.

"I kind of slipped up and told Slaid. He wouldn't tell anybody. But, I know (Cross' daughter) Charlie, and she couldn't hold a secret. She'd be calling everybody. They're happy, but Charlie is still kind of in disbelief. They're getting to do some fun stuff, I'll tell you that."

Ultimately, that "fun stuff" would be Charlie Cross kicking off the song "Boys From Oklahoma" at all four Boys From Oklahoma concerts by playing the introduction on harmonica, after Cody Canada told 48,000 people, "Charlie has something she wants to say to y'all."

It became the moment that defined the week of Ragweed's return. First inconceivable, it took on a feeling of destiny by the time the four men set foot on the stage at Boone Pickens Stadium and took their victory laps.

"I guess a lot of people missed us, and we missed them," Cross says. "I truly did."

NEVER SAY NEVER

Slaid and Grady Cross play with Cody Canada and the Departed in November 2024 at the Joe State Tailgate at Eskimo Joe's during Oklahoma State's Homecoming weekend.

GRADY CROSS

Cody Canada and Grady Cross at Cain's Ballroom in Tulsa in March 2025.

NEVER SAY NEVER

Randy Ragsdale

For most of his life, music, to Randy Ragsdale, has meant Cross Canadian Ragweed and nothing else.

"Oh shit, this is gonna sound stupid," he says, "but there's something there that you can't get by playing with anyone else. I don't even know how to describe it, but it's just a natural feel, and a natural energy that comes out when I play with Plato and Cody and Grady. I've played with others a lot, and there's always just that something missing, you know? It just definitely feels like there's something bigger than us up there playing.

"Even now. Our first rehearsal, when we got up there after 15 years, we just busted them out, one after the next. It's just easy for us."

That feeling is the natural result of a decade and a half setting — and achieving — goals higher than any artist in Red Dirt had dared to pursue before, building diehard fanbases far from Oklahoma. Far-flung locales like Chicago and Birmingham and Phoenix became hotbeds for Ragweed fandom, and sold-out shows in rock rooms and theaters around the country stood as evidence of the band's mass appeal in its 2000s prime.

"That was the high of being on the road, you know?" Ragsdale says. "It was an adrenaline high. Being on the road and traveling like we did at the level we did it at for all those years was pretty much impossible. What made it possible was that feeling that you get when you play shows where everyone is singing the songs back to you. You can put up with the rest of the hours in the day, because you get those two hours at night. You feel accomplished, like you're doing something right. It's not all for nothing, then."

More than anything, that enthusiasm from Ragsdale is what set the entire tone for the band. When the group came together as teenagers, it was Ragsdale who provided them with a place to practice. More specifically, it was Ragsdale's father, the late Johnny C. Ragsdale — himself a musician — who provided them with a place to practice. Cody Canada fondly recalls the group setting up in Ragsdale's living room one Super Bowl Sunday and working through songs during the game.

"I wanted to play The Wormy Dog, man," Ragsdale says of those days. "We were in high school. We would go play high school parties, or tailgate parties out in the country. We figured out pretty quick, 'Man, we maybe oughta set our goals a little higher.' But honestly, we would just play for whoever would listen, and that was it."

What he found was that just about everybody would listen.

"Man. I think it was the good old days," Ragsdale says. "When you think of Bruce Springsteen singing 'Glory Days' or shit like that, those were the days for me and our band. But, we were super grateful to be there and just get to do it. Because, we weren't any more special than a million other bands out there, we were lucky to be able to do it. I was super thankful that people cared that much, and we had chances to do that.

"But it kept building. I had a goal. My dad told me, 'When you play Billy Bob's, that's making it.' So, when we played Billy Bob's, that was a huge, monumental day for me. I was like, 'Man. What's after this?' Then, you realize you just want to keep going and see how far we can go."

The band's 2010 split, at the time, was chalked up to Ragsdale's desire to get off the road and care for his son, JC, who was born with a severe form of epilepsy. There was some truth to it, but it masked deeper divisions within the group that were the primary factor in the breakup. When it happened, the same "Ragweed or nothing" attitude led Ragsdale to backburner music entirely.

"I wanted to put space between myself and everything that I'd been doing, and just have time to process and think," he says. "It was a tough decision to want to leave everything that I had going on. But, at the same time, it felt inevitable, and I just wanted to save whatever I could.

"I made that happen with the idea that I'll figure it out when I get there. Right now, I just want some time and space. And, not much longer after that, I started finding myself being outside working with trees, anything to get out and stretch and think. I thought I'd get back to music eventually, but I ran the other way."

"I thought I wanted to leave it exactly as it was, and then maybe one day I'd get back to it and get to do it again."

It turned out to be JC — and his sister, Julia — who kept music alive in Ragsdale's life for most of the 15 years that followed.

"It wasn't a part of our daily life for Dad to be in music," he says, "but there was a lot of stories and reminiscing. Kids asking questions, watching old footage and making fun of Dad. My son, JC, literally almost every single day, he would pull out his iPad and watch us. Usually, it was the one from Cain's. There was a lot of that. They always wanted me to tell stories. Music was alive, but it wasn't something I did as a job anymore."

He did not totally abandon the drum kit. He briefly toured with Stoney LaRue, and he had a run with Cross in 2019 in a Yukon-based band they called Cross, Rags and Young, but it was, at best, a hobby to Ragsdale. His career had moved to the oil fields. His personal life involved getting married for the second time. Along with being a parent to JC and Julia, he became a stepdad to the children of his wife, Jamie. He had a family, and music was on the outer edges of his life.

A phone call in summer 2024 snapped him out of that.

"I had just got home from work. I was sitting in my driveway, finishing up some paperwork on my computer in my truck, and I got a phone call from Neil Jay, our accountant," Ragsdale says now. "I hadn't talked to that guy in a decade. I went, 'What's the Ragweed accountant calling for?' So, I let it go to voicemail, because I needed to be real coherent for whatever that was. I was a little scattered.

"He left a message, and I listened to it, and it was, like, the most vague goddamn thing I ever heard in my life. I was like, 'Really?' He was saying, 'There's this great thing that could be a big deal, but the problem is that I can't tell you what it is.' So, I was like, 'OK. You got my attention.' And I called him back. He asked for Grady's number, and he set up a dinner with us."

At the dinner, Jay — himself an Oklahoma State graduate — and Ragweed's agent Jon Folk laid out a proposal: The band would get back together and perform a show at Boone Pickens Stadium. After that, they'd see what happens.

"I was shocked, super shocked," Ragsdale says. "And, it took a minute for anything to sink in. Are we back? Are we doing one show? What are we even talking about? Where's this headed? But, I think everybody wanted to baby step into it, that was the only way it would work. We were all a little gun shy. But, from where we sit today? It's all gone extremely smooth. I don't see why we wouldn't want to do more."

"Today," in this case, is a bar on Duval Street in Key West, where all of Ragweed gathered in January 2025 for a mini-reunion at Mile 0 Fest. At that point, the slight hesitation that came with the first invitation had given way to a brotherhood. The band members had spoken to one another, caught up, and were friends again.

That part happened over two nights — Halloween weekend 2024 — when the four members of Ragweed were invited to Homecoming weekend at OSU. They first gathered at Eskimo Joe's on Friday night, where The Departed headlined the annual Joe State Tailgate parking lot party. Eventually, Cross would step on stage and play guitar on a song.

The next day, all of Ragweed, plus friends and family, were introduced to the crowd at the Cowboy football game at Boone Pickens Stadium. When public address announcer Larry Reece introduced them, the cheer was louder than any that the actual game itself would draw.

The group watched the game in the suite of university president Kayse Shrum. Ragsdale's son, JC, was there. When Canada saw him taking in the atmosphere, he quietly broke down in tears.

"I don't want to keep saying it was the beginning of something, but it was," Ragsdale says of Homecoming. "It was the beginning of Ragweed's second part. It was our kids getting to meet. It was my new wife getting to meet everybody. It was putting us all in one room, and it was super refreshing, because we all had fun.

"If it was just about our kids, that would be enough. That's it, for me."

Less than a month later, JC Ragsdale passed away. He was 25. Ragsdale and his family were devastated, but they and the band emerged from the funeral and weeks of mourning resolved to dedicate The Boys From Oklahoma weekend to JC.

"No matter what I've got going on in life, it could always be worse," Ragsdale says of JC. "You cherish a lot of the simple things that a lot of people take for granted. You pay attention to what matters, and you just fucking learn how to soften up and have a heart, because some people have a hard fight just to get through the day. One little thing that you might think is small might mean the whole world to someone else.

"I didn't realize what an impact Ragweed had on my own son until I came home. For the last 15 years, he was just watching videos of us over and over again."

There's a cruelty to it, but Ragsdale has been the face of loss throughout Ragweed's time as a band. His father, Johnny, died of cancer in 1997 — prompting Canada and Cross to write "Johnny's Song" and Randy to write "Daddy's at Home" for the band's 2001 record, *Highway 377*. His younger sister, Mandi, died as a result of a car wreck returning from a Ragweed concert in College Station, Texas, in 2001. Then, as with JC's passing, Ragweed formed an important part of Ragsdale's comfort blanket. That comfort extended to Ragsdale's family, including his mother, Ruth Ann Ragsdale, and helped Randy find something adjacent to peace through his family's grief.

"I think they all just loved the music, the band," he says. "We all shared that. Dad just instilled that inside of me. I'll carry that forever from him. Without him, I wouldn't be playing music at all. For Mandi and JC, it was the love of the music, and that was an extension of him, too. It all really comes down to the music, I think."

Through that pain, Ragsdale became a musician again. He rehearsed relentlessly with the band and on his own time. He quit his oil field job ahead of the reunion. When he found himself on the verge of the concerts, he was locked in. Cross Canadian Ragweed's drummer was ready.

"I am super, super excited. There's a whole lot of feelings," he said ahead of the shows. "That's been 15 years. That's a whole lot of time, and a whole lot of life. There was so much thinking that it would never happen again, and here we are. I feel like we've all grown up and learned about ourselves. Maybe this is just like a second chance to get to do this, and to do it right. I'm extremely grateful for the chance to get to do that at all. It seemed so impossible for so many years. For it to be here now, I can't believe it's actually happening.

"Plus, my family and my kids remember that. It meant a lot to my son, and it makes me happy to be able to do this in his honor, and to do it for him."

NEVER SAY NEVER

Randy Ragsdale on the drum kit for Cross Canadian Ragweed at Cain's Ballroom in March 2025.

RANDY RAGSDALE

NEVER SAY NEVER

Jeremy Plato

"In the back of my mind, I always thought that it might just happen."

Jeremy Plato was always the outlier of the group. After 15 years on the bass for Ragweed, Plato jumped in the pocket for Cody Canada and The Departed in 2010 and has spent another 15 years — and counting — in that band.

But he was also the one member of Ragweed who viewed a reunion as a matter of when, not if.

"I think it was maybe just a couple of years ago," Plato recalls, "that Cody started asking me, 'What would it be like if we just, like, did a couple of shows, you know?' And I went, 'You know me, man. I'm down to do whatever.' Like I said, I always thought it was bound to happen."

That's who Plato is. He cuts a calm and cool figure while his compatriots in both bands rock their brains out, but he's acutely observant, and he's been perceptive of his bandmates — in particular, Canada himself.

"Being a father, he has witnessed and used methods of letting things go or lightening up," Plato says of Canada. "He's not hanging on to things that are toxic and that can hurt you. I think that's what happened, really."

He's referencing the personal changes he has observed in Canada as the two men aged and matured alongside each other in two bands over the span of three decades. But, we're in the back lounge of The De-

JEREMY PLATO

parted's bus at Mile 0 Fest in January, and he's also cutting a satisfied figure as Ragweed's comeback takes shape.

Reflecting on the day he learned the reunion was on, Plato says, "I remember my internal personal reaction was, 'HA! I KNEW IT!' And then, out loud, I was like, 'I'm fucking down, bro. Let's do this.'

"Now? Two words — holy shit. I thought it would be big, but I didn't know it would be that big. I really didn't. I had thought that, when the band broke up and it was all over with, well, that's that. But I also thought that maybe we could get back together and do some shows. But, when it happened, the reaction to it, from the fans and everybody else, blew me away.

"Then, my mind went directly to, we're gonna have to sound like we never fucking stopped."

Plato joined Ragweed a year or so after the group formed in 1994 in Yukon, Oklahoma. He's the lone member who is not part of the mash-up that forms the band's name because of this. Count yourself lucky in this aspect, or you'd be reading a book about the triumphant comeback of Cross Canadian Ragplate, which, let's face it, is not a good name.

Plato hails from Calumet, Oklahoma, but he grew up in Yukon and knew Canada, Grady Cross and Randy Ragsdale in high school. He harbored musical aspirations even when he was making ends meet driving trucks.

"This is no bullshit," Plato recalls. "I was at my best friend's house. We were celebrating my birthday, and I made a birthday wish. My birthday wish was to get in a band, and actually go somewhere with it somehow, because I was a truck driver then. And then, it happened! Within a year, it happened.

"When I got with these guys, I thought that they were serious and wanted to be serious about it. So I put big boy pants on and went, *let's fucking do this*."

When Ragweed went out and did it, things happened fast. Looking back now at Ragweed's early-2000s heyday, Plato wishes he'd have slowed down and taken it all in more than he did.

"It was kind of a blur, to be quite honest with you," he says. "In those days, it was almost non-stop touring, playing gig after gig after gig. And then, 'Oh! We have these recording dates! So, let's do a two-week block of recording in the studio, and then we'll have two or three shows after that, and then we can go home."

One thing Plato was always aware of, however, was the intangible "X-factor" that Ragweed has. He says it's the reason playing bass in the group comes so naturally to him.

"I can usually tell by at least song two that I think we're gonna be fine," he says of Ragweed shows. "From there, confidence is already up, so you can just do whatever. If you're feeling froggy, pull your pants down. That's just kind of how it goes. If it all goes off without a hitch, and it usually does, it's *all* good."

That feeling is also why he stuck with Canada post-Ragweed and devoted the second half of his career to The Departed.

"Personally? To be quite honest, as far as I was concerned, it wasn't, like back to the drawing board. It was, 'Practice some more, asshole.' And that was it," he says of Ragweed's 2010 split. "So, when I got asked the question by Cody, what do we do? I was like, 'Let's start another band. This is what I do. I'm pretty sure it's what you do.'"

"I was heartbroken when the band broke up, but at the same time, I was bound and determined to do this again. As long as it involved me playing bass or singing, it was gonna happen."

He got the same feeling when he learned Ragweed would play again, though he credits Oklahoma State's 2024 Homecoming weekend — when all four members of Ragweed met in person for the first time since their breakup and were honored as guests of then-university president Kayse Shrum at the football game — with helping him feel like it was real again.

That experience also let him wrap his mind around playing four concerts in the same stadium.

"I've never been a, like, stage fright type of person," Plato says. "But, it is scary! And, anxious at the same time, like, '*This is gonna be fucking cool. The best damn crowds ever.*'"

JEREMY PLATO

Cody Canada and The Departed, with Jeremy Plato on bass, in November 2024.

JEREMY PLATO

NEVER SAY NEVER

Cody Canada

Two days before The Boys From Oklahoma concerts began, Cody Canada found himself impatient, sitting in the living room of a house he had rented for the week in Stillwater, half a mile from Boone Pickens Stadium. Sound check was a few hours away. The next day would truly be a free day, at least until all of Ragweed — and all of Waves in April, the metal band that both of Canada's sons, Dierks and Willy, play in, would gather for dinner at Eskimo Joes, partly as a chance to chill in Stillwater's destination restaurant and partly to celebrate Willy's 17th birthday.

This morning, though, all Canada had to do was think … and maybe overthink.

"It's slightly frightening," he says. The first Ragweed concert is still 30 hours out. "Especially, getting everything set up and seeing the floor tiling in place. Good Lord, it's big."

Ragweed was on the verge of completing the comeback, of course. But it also marked a comeback for Canada, too. A year earlier, he had said "never" about the prospect of a reunion. Today, he was proud to eat those words. He would head to sound check — and perform all four nights — with guitar picks that featured the Ragweed logo on one side and The Departed logo on the other. "Two bands. I can do that now," he bragged.

It even marked a long way from July 2024, when he first entertained, then accepted, the offer to reunite the Red Dirt icons in Stillwater. A few weeks later, agent Jon Folk had all of Ragweed on board.

"I remember it being so uneasy," Canada says now with a smirk, "just thinking about what we have to do to make this work, and thinking, 'What if we don't?' I honestly thought we would sell about 20,000 tickets, and that would be about it. But, once everything started working, it started rolling so easily.'

"We talked about no drinking and how we wanted to do this like we were *supposed* to do it, and how we might not ever get to do it again.

"Looking back on it, watching all of the people that have helped and the people that have donated their time, if I had the list in front of me and read it word-for-word, I still wouldn't be able to thank everybody. It's amazing sitting down and looking out across everybody. I just think about that call from Jon saying *everybody's in*."

Nobody pulled more of that weight than Shannon Canada. She's Cody's wife, but she is also the only manager Ragweed has ever known. Some time around 1998, when she and Cody were living in Stillwater and dating, the band handed over their lockbox full of everything they had to Shannon, and she has been in charge since.

That meant coordinating Ragweed's portion of The Boys From Oklahoma fell to her, and Cody had a front-row seat.

"I was joking with Shannon when we pulled into town yesterday," he said. "I went, 'Man. I don't feel so good,' and she went, 'Don't you even *try* it.'

"I sat on the other side of the kitchen bar at home, watching her go through all this. There's days that I would see her want to pull her hair out. But, there's also days that she'll just start crying, because people will send her messages that say things like, 'My kids didn't get a chance to see the band, and now I'm going to be with my kids, and we'll be able to have a beer together.' It's pretty incredible.

"Watching her do it alone — she's not 100 percent alone, but other bands have multiple people to do this job. Every day of my life, I say I'm proud of her, but watching her pull off what other people have a team to do is pretty awesome."

For Shannon's part, the concert planning was a new and arduous task, but it did not bother her.

"I have had lots of help from people that I trust," Shannon says. "Turnpike has a gal that works for them who has taught me a ton of stuff about the merchandising side of an event like this. That was probably my biggest hurdle, because I had never done anything like that. I mean, I can plan a party! And, the Midway festival outside the stadium was Kyle Carter, but I just needed the bodies to help me do it, because our staff is literally me and my brother at home."

The hard part, Shannon explains, was *getting* to the point that there was even a concert to plan. She was the one who fielded the first call from Kyle Waters proposing the comeback, and she was the one who had to tell Waters "fuck no" at the end of it. Ragweed's breakup 15 years earlier still stung both her and Cody, and a reunion remained a nonstarter even as offers became nearly impossible to ignore. But, in 2022, the Turnpike Troubadours reunited after a three-year break, and their comeback shows at Cain's Ballroom in Tulsa and Red Rocks Amphitheatre outside of Denver drew upwards of 70,000 fans to ticket queues, crashing websites and causing a firestorm on social media. Amid the storm, comments like "imagine what a Ragweed comeback would do" stuck around.

That fall, the Canadas and their children spent Thanksgiving in New York. They got a hotel room overlooking the Macy's Thanksgiving Day Parade route. Their close friends, Jimmy "Taco" and Kari Flex, along with their children, joined them. I was there, too. Thanksgiving dinner was hosted in my living room in upper Manhattan. My two-year-old mix of Rottweiler, Chow Chow, German shepherd, and Chihuahua — Rosalie — was particularly infatuated with Dierks Canada during dinner. Afterward, the adults went out to a bar on Manhattan's Lower East Side that was serving holiday-themed cocktails. Despite (or perhaps because of) the holiday, we had a corner of the bar to ourselves. As the evening drew on, cocktails and jokes gave way to sentiment, and Cody and Shannon shared a moment.

"I just had a random thought like, 'What are our long-term goals?' Just like a little game you do in your head," Shannon said. "And, Cody started to cry. I just knew, because — obviously — I knew him. But, that's when I could see that he was open to it."

Nearly two years — and one ill-fated *Rolling Stone* story in which Cody said "never" for the final time — later, Shannon saw what a tale of redemption looks like.

"In our household, it primarily was a huge weight that you could see was lifted off of Cody's shoulders," she says.

Ragweed gathered often between the October announcement and April concerts. Sometimes, they'd rehearse in Fort Worth, at the rehearsal space of the Toadies' Vaden Todd Lewis. There was also JC Ragsdale's funeral. There was Mile 0 Fest in Key West, when Ragweed played six songs together for the first time since 2010. There was the Oklahoma Music Hall of Fame surprise in March. Shannon flew in at the last minute to watch the hall crash a Departed show to inform Ragweed of their impending induction.

But it was the 2024 Oklahoma State Homecoming weekend that Shannon says made Ragweed a family again.

"The first moment when we saw Grady and Randy at Homecoming, and you knew that it really was *back*," she says. "It didn't feel like 15 years had passed."

By the time the shows rolled around, Shannon's work was largely done. Tour managers, crew members, and a massive production team could take it from here. With her schedule now clear enough to anticipate the first concert, she only had one thing on her mind.

"I'm looking forward to going down into the pit and watching the show."

She shared that sentiment with the 48,000 other people who would file into Boone Pickens Stadium over the next four nights. The day before Ragweed's downbeat, that was where Cody Canada's mind kept returning. This comeback was only a resounding success in hindsight. Everybody, Ragweed included, underestimated just how much of a mark they had left.

Now, it was time to see it all pay off.

"It was just amazing to me to see that people still listen," Cody Canada says. "The younger musicians from Texas really have stood out a lot, because they keep sending me Instagram messages that say 'FOUR DAYS OUT' and I'm thinking, 'You weren't even *walking* when we split up.'

"I don't know. There is a moment where I can say that I am speechless sometimes, because I don't have anything to pull together. I'm afraid that I'll just completely fall to pieces for 10 minutes and cry all over the stage, you know?"

Cody Canada and The Departed play in Las Vegas in December 2022.

CODY CANADA

Cody Canada at Eskimo Joe's in Stillwater, Oklahoma, in April 2018. (Clay Billman)

Boone Pickens Stadium | Stillwater, Oklahoma

Roughly three decades ago, four guys from right here in Stillwater, Oklahoma, came together and formed a band with a sound that would help define the Red Dirt music genre.

As we can all see, it's as true today as it was 30 years ago. If these guys are in town, that's where everyone is going to be.

And tonight, we got 'em back: Cody Canada, Grady Cross, Randy Ragsdale and Jeremy Plato.

Oklahoma State University welcomes Cross Canadian Ragweed!

Mike Gundy, Oklahoma State University football coach, introducing the band

NEVER SAY NEVER

Night One: 4.10.25

With Cross Canadian Ragweed due on stage in less than five minutes, Chris McCoy had a message for Cody Canada.

McCoy has handled front-of-house sound for Ragweed from day one, literally making the leap from house sound engineer at The Wormy Dog Saloon to his position with Ragweed in 2001, when the band first grew into the need for their own crew. McCoy moved to The Randy Rogers Band after Ragweed's 2010 split, but he was back in his old role for The Boys From Oklahoma shows, and from backstage, he yelled, "Hey Cods!" over the heads of the gathered friends, family, and crew members still readying the stage and lines for Ragweed.

In the frenzy, he had to say it a second time. "Hey, Cods!"

Canada turned around this time.

"Love you," McCoy told the frontman, before he went back to engineering the show 48,000 people were moments away from taking in.

Then, Ragweed sized up the expectations — months of comeback hype, a stadium filled with fans doing the wave, a five-band lineup of Red Dirt icons, and an introduction by Oklahoma State University football coach Mike Gundy — and finally, after walking out to Taylor Swift's "We Are Never Ever Getting Back Together," made a collective decision to blow right past them.

The Oklahoma four-piece credited with laying the groundwork for today's soaring popularity of Red Dirt music capped a layoff of near-

NIGHT ONE

ly 15 years on Thursday night with a blistering two-and-a-half-hour comeback concert at Boone Pickens Stadium in Stillwater — the town where they got their start and paid their dues 30 years ago.

"It seems like it was a really long time ago, and not six or seven months ago, that we were talking about how we were gonna do this," Canada told the sellout crowd. "Now we're here. We fucking did it."

Canada delighted in reminding the crowd that Ragweed's last show in Stillwater had come in 2010, at the famed Calf Fry festival at the Tumbleweed Dance Hall. That show ended with Canada taking a liquor bottle to the head, which had been thrown from the crowd. "We come in peace!" he said on Thursday. "Don't throw anything at me!"

Ragweed followed a scorching set from co-headliners the Turnpike Troubadours, plus shows from The Great Divide, Jason Boland and The Stragglers, and Stoney Larue, at the first night of The Boys From Oklahoma.

Canada, along with Grady Cross, Jeremy Plato and Randy Ragsdale, spent the weeks ahead of the concert raking in accolades, including an induction into The Oklahoma Music Hall of Fame and the Icon Award from Texas Music & Radio Awards. Thursday night, they turned the fervor on its head with what should go down as the most memorable concert in the state's history.

By the time Ragweed stepped into the spotlight Thursday night, the concert had already cemented its place in Red Dirt lore. From the start, the show was steeped in Red Dirt history. LaRue opened with his version of "Oklahoma Breakdown," the Mike Hosty-penned tune that was 2007's best-selling single in Texas, and he followed it with a cover of the Red Dirt Rangers' "Idabel Blues," with the Red Dirt Rangers joining in.

Boland followed with a set heavy on the songs he wrote when he lived in this town, such as "Pearl Snaps" and "Proud Souls." The Great Divide led off the third set — by which time the crowd had completely filled the stadium — with "College Days," which McClure wrote about Stillwater.

When the Turnpike Troubadours are in their element, they are one of the hardest bands in country music to follow. Thursday night, they were in their element. The co-headliners played a stomping, high-energy show for 70 minutes with a setlist filled with enough Turnpike standards that it effectively dared Ragweed to try to top it.

"How does it feel to be a part of the biggest night in Oklahoma music ever?" Felker asked the crowd. "All of the bands on this stage are the reason we get to do this. I've had a lot of great nights in my life, but this is the best one ever."

Turnpike has half a dozen staples, and on this night, "Good Lord Lorrie" and their cover of John Hartford's "Long, Hot Summer Day" brought the first real stadium-rattling cheers from the audience.

The Troubadours finished with "Heaven Passing Through," the focus track from their brand-new album, *The Price of Admission*, before ceding the stage to Cross Canadian Ragweed with the bar set extremely high.

Front and center, on the rail, stood Eli Jordan, decked out in Oklahoma State orange. Jordan, native to Verdigris, Oklahoma, was the first person in line at Boone Pickens Stadium's Gate 4 that morning, showing up around 9:30 a.m. and waiting six-and-a-half hours for the 4 p.m. opening of doors. Himself a recent college graduate — 2023 from McPherson, to be exact — Jordan has made himself at home in Red Dirt circles, both as a fan and as a musician himself. On this day, he was bound and determined to take in his first-ever Ragweed show from the best spot in the stadium.

"I'm excited," Jordan said beforehand. "I moved away and went to college in Kansas, and I got into Turnpike and Ragweed. And, four years ago, I never thought I'd ever see either of them. Here I am seeing both of them — along with Boland, Stoney, and The Great Divide. I'm feeling like, 'Holy shit! How are we all here together?'

"They're the reason we have Oklahoma music as we know it today."

Ultimately, it would not have mattered if The Beatles went on before Ragweed, because the night belonged to the garage band from Stillwater.

Ragweed played an hour longer than their planned set time. At one point, Canada pleaded with event organizers from the mic, "Y'all, don't shut us off! We haven't played a show in 16 fucking years."

Ragweed did not just burn through their catalog, though. They laid bare for all in attendance the driving forces behind their comeback.

The children whose own musical pursuits spurred the comeback all made it on stage, highlighted by Charlie Cross, who stepped to center stage with a harmonica to kick off the event's title song, "Boys From Oklahoma." That brought the loudest roar of the night and surely rivaled some of the stadium's biggest football games for the all-time decibel record — all the while accentuated by heavy green lights courtesy of production director Willard Kendall that turned the usually-orange stadium into a sea of 420 green. The Red Dirt Rangers, along with the song's writer, Gene Collier, contributed improv verses to the song.

There was a steady stream of special guests throughout the night. Dierks Bentley joined to sing his favorite Ragweed song, "42 Miles," and needed a second chance to pick up a musical cue because he was busy being a fan, taking pics of Ragweed and the crowd from the stage as though he was not a veteran of such a vantage point. It was a reminder that, before Bentley and Ragweed set off on half a decade worth of "High Times and Hangovers" tours, Bentley was such a fan of Ragweed that he approached the band at a Nashville show — when Bentley was still mostly an unknown musician — to tell them how cool they were.

Felker sat in for a verse of "Brooklyn Kid," Boland did the same on "17," and Wade Bowen sang "Constantly." Before kicking off "Carney Man" — the kitschy circus tune Canada and McClure wrote that put Ragweed on the map in the late 1990s — Canada smirked to the crowd, "This is what you wanted!"

The night ended with a cover of Reckless Kelly's "Crazy Eddie's Last Hurrah," with Willy and Cody Braun from Reckless contributing on vocals and mandolin, respectively. The song itself is a fictional tale about a murder of passion, but fans sang the final chorus loudly and clearly, as though the lyrics were plausible to at least a few.

Then, Ragweed walked off the stage. Spouses, children and fellow artists met all four men at the end of the stage with a mix of laughter and tears, along with an endless line of hugs. Canada cut through the euphoria just long enough to put the evening into words.

"What a good fucking time," he said.

Cross Canadian Ragweed Setlist: Night 1
Anywhere But Here; Lonely Girl; Sister; Leave Me Alone; Long Way Home; To Find My Love (Turner Bruton cover, Jeremy Plato singing); Constantly w/Wade Bowen; In Oklahoma; Broken; The Years; Bang My Head; Soul Agent (Scott Evans cover, Jeremy Plato singing);

Carney Man w/Mike McClure; 17 w/Jason Boland; Pay; On a Cloud; Brooklyn Kid w/Evan Felker; Wanna Rock and Roll (Ray Wylie Hubbard cover); Cry Lonely w/Shelby Stone; Sick and Tired w/Graycie York; 42 Miles w/Dierks Bentley; Alabama w/Stoney LaRue; Boys From Oklahoma (Gene Collier cover); Don't Need You; Late Last Night (Todd Snider cover); Crazy Eddie's Last Hurrah (Reckless Kelly cover) w/Willy and Cody Braun.

Turnpike Troubadours Setlist: Night 1
Mean Old Sun; Brought Me; The Bird Hunters; Kansas City Southern; Gin, Smoke, Lies; Before the Devil Knows We're Dead; House Fire; Whole Damn Town; Good Lord Lorrie; 7&7; Every Girl; The Mercury; Diamonds and Gasoline; Unrung; Pay No Rent; Long Hot Summer Day (John Hartford cover); Heaven Passing Through

NIGHT ONE

The crowd watches Cross Canadian Ragweed during their Thursday night performance.

The view from sidestage as Ragweed headlines for the first time in 15 years.

Fans at Boone Pickens Stadium take in Ragweed's Thursday night set.

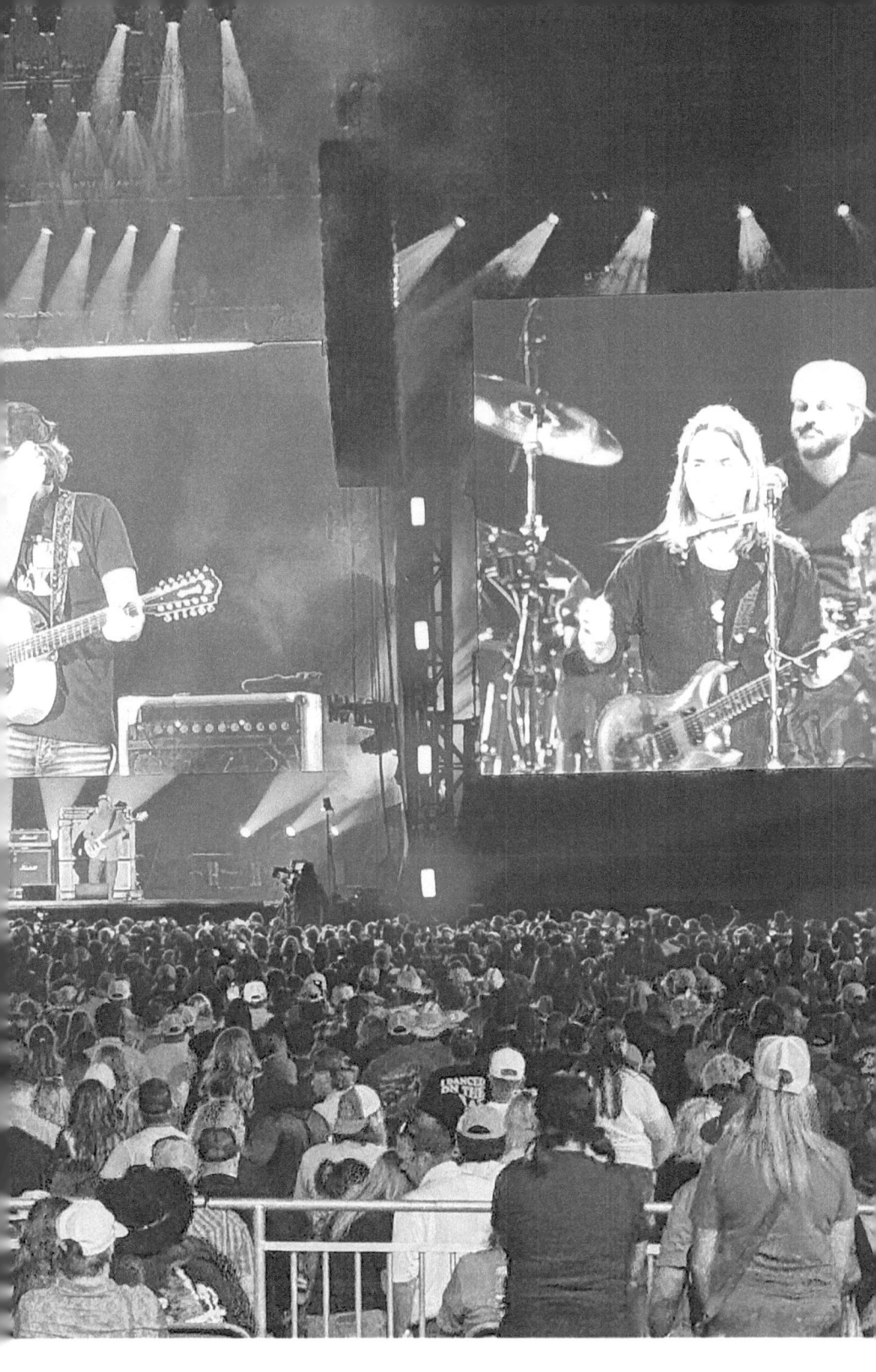

Dierks Bentley takes a photo from the stage on Thursday night. (Clay Billman)

Stoney LaRue plays the first song of The Boys From Oklahoma on Thursday.

The Great Divide play before a full stadium on Thursday night.

The Turnpike Troubadours kick off their Boys From Oklahoma run with "Mean Old Sun."

The spectacle for The Turnpike Troubadours on Thursday night.

NEVER SAY NEVER

Night Two: 4.11.25

For mid-April, at least, Friday brought a hot, breezy day to Stillwater. It was, technically, a school day at Oklahoma State, but for the most part, garnering an education and preparing to be the leaders of tomorrow gave way to the second day of Red Dirt Woodstock, and the first one that felt like an all-day party. Tailgates popped up around campus, and live music kicked off all over town before noon. The Tumbleweed had two stages and got going over the lunch hour. Eskimo Joe's was packed all day, and Washington Street south of campus — The Strip — had a gameday atmosphere from the get-go.

Friday was also the only day that The Boys From Oklahoma lineup changed. Members of The Great Divide had prior commitments when the shows were extended from one day to four, so in their place, The Mike McClure Band kicked off the show inside Boone Pickens Stadium shortly after 5 p.m.

McClure made a name for himself fronting The Great Divide, but it's with The Mike McClure Band where he recorded the bulk of his catalog. In the process of crafting the concerts, Cody Canada insisted on MMB replacing The Great Divide on this night. It allowed people like Eric Hansen — drummer for both Cody Canada and The Departed and MMB, as well as an Oklahoma State alumnus — and Caleb Shirtum — bass player for both MMB and The Damn Quails, and McClure's son-in-law — to take the stage at Boone Pickens Stadium. It also allowed McClure to sell a t-shirt that immediately became a hit at the merch

NIGHT TWO

tables. On the front was the band's logo. The back read, "Mike McClure Band: Stadium Tour 2025" followed by the phrase "April 11th, Boone Pickens Stadium, Stillwater, OK" repeating continually until it filled the back out.

When it came time for MMB to play, Canada himself gave the group its intro, but not before warning the crowd, "You know we're gonna go over time tonight, right?" in reference to the previous night that busted curfew by a full hour.

"All roads lead to this next gentleman," Canada said about McClure. "He took a whole bunch of us young ones and believed in us. He told us either, 'That's a real good song,' or, 'Don't ever play that again.' But it was all love."

With that, the stadium stage came alive for its second act.

The only constant between The Mike McClure Band and The Great Divide is McClure himself. MMB is a rock band where The Divide is country at every turn. So when McClure delivered staples like "Out in the Fields," "I Am Not Broken," and "The Void," they were true one-off moments for the rapidly-gathering crowd. McClure's partner and half of acoustic duo Crow and Gazelle, Chrislyn Lawrence, sat in as well during the half-hour opening set.

As the order of the first three bands rotated each night, Stoney LaRue found himself up next, and for the second night in a row, he kicked his set off with "Oklahoma Breakdown" before tearing through half an hour of his best-known songs. When he sang "Down in Flames," he told the crowd, "Sing it loud, Stillwater" and got what he wanted.

When LaRue got around to "One Chord Song," the simple tune — it's a D chord, if you have ever wondered — turned into an extended jam in which Canada as well as LaRue's son, C.J., came on stage to lend some more guitars to the band.

Jason Boland and The Stragglers landed in the "direct to Turnpike" spot on both Nights 2 and 3, and on this one, they were heavy on Oklahoma tunes. "If I Ever Get Back to Oklahoma" was the first song on their setlist, and they went back to the well midway through their show with the Danny Flowers-penned "Tulsa Time."

The Stragglers released a new album, *The Last Kings of Babylon*, in March, and Boland gave fans a taste of it near the end of his set with "The Next to Last Hank Williams."

NEVER SAY NEVER

Friday marked the only night of the week that start times moved up half an hour, meaning that the Turnpike Troubadours played the first half hour of their co-headlining set facing into the setting sun. What they lost in the production — Turnpike's stadium show is full-bore, complete with a tiered stage and major incorporation of both video and lights that are best viewed at night — they made up for in the poetry of kicking off their show with "Mean Old Sun" opposite the real sun. During the song, a clearly-joyous Evan Felker made his way around the stage and up on the top tier alongside his bandmates, a major departure from the norm for Felker, who generally opts to play his show front and center, behind his mic, a la George Strait. But the excitement of a second-straight packed house overcame him.

"Stillwater, Oklahoma, how ya doing?" Felker asked once "Mean Old Sun" finished. "This is the second night of the biggest music festival in Oklahoma history!"

Aside from a pause midway through "The Bird Hunters" when a fan in the general admission pit required medical assistance — prompting Felker to remind fans to hydrate — Turnpike nailed their second show of the week.

Felker embraced the moment and made several references to Stillwater over the 70-minute set. He switched the climatic line in "Before the Devil Knows We're Dead" to say, "Tell everyone in Stillwater I love you all to death," and he added "I can sing those Jason Boland songs" to "Whole Damn Town."

When Felker and Hank Early played a pared-down version of "Diamonds and Gasoline," most of the stadium lights went down while fans turned their phone lights on and waved them in rhythm, prompting Felker to remark, "That's really pretty" mid-song.

Like Thursday night, the crowd could have left happy if everything had ended with Turnpike, but like Thursday night, the crowd still had the little matter of a two-and-a-half-hour Ragweed set to come. Backstage as the set changed over from Turnpike's to Ragweed's, the band members were loose and enjoying the moment. There had been some nerves the night before, but this night was shaping up to be an all-out rock show.

The members of Ragweed are a far cry from their partying days as a band, and they all agreed that they would avoid alcohol before any

NIGHT TWO

of their sets. (Obviously, Grady Cross, nearly a decade sober, avoided it throughout.) Shortly before Ragweed's downbeat, Randy Ragsdale cracked a smile and relished playing with a clear head.

"I gotta earn my beer tonight," he said as he looked at the 48,000 strong waiting around for Ragweed.

When the walk-out music — "Walk" by Pantera — kicked in, Canada started jumping around on the side of the stage, feeling the energy of the evening. Ragweed then matched the tone of their walk-out song by leading off with "Number" and its raucous "1-2-3-4" callback from the stadium crowd.

Canada was openly appreciative of Stillwater from start to finish all week, but it was clearly on his mind Friday. "Stillwater! Night 2!" was all he said after the first song finished, but he returned to the theme over and over throughout:

"We're back in the town that gave us all we got," he said before bringing up The Smokin' Oaks — including Slaid Cross — to play "Suicide Blues."

Before playing "Bang My Head" Canada pointed out that he wrote the song after hours at Shortcakes Diner, the staple of late-night breakfast and late-morning hangover cures in Stillwater.

At the end of "17," which once again featured Jason Boland singing a verse, Canada sang, "I'm Stillwater bound."

He told the crowd, "We're gonna start rolling out the Red Dirt heroes. Is that alright?" before a veritable parade of Red Dirt legends came on stage over the course of half a dozen songs. The Red Dirt Rangers and Gene Collier reprised their verses on "Boys From Oklahoma" late in the set, once again with the stadium bathed in green light and a 420-themed video playing behind the stage.

The night before, Evan Felker had joined Canada for an acoustic rendition of "Brooklyn Kid," but with the song out of the setlist on the second night, Felker opted instead to join McClure for the song that put Ragweed on the map, "Carney Man."

The night ended with a two-song encore. First up was "Don't Need You," and featuring Bear Plato — Jeremy's son — filling in on bass. For the second night in a row, Willy Braun joined Ragweed for the finale, a cover of Reckless Kelly's fictional tale of murder, "Crazy Eddie's Last Hurrah."

A pair of long days were in the books, and if the week had ended right then, it would already have gone down as the biggest musical event in Oklahoma history. As it stood, though, we were only halfway done.

Cross Canadian Ragweed Setlist: Night 2
Number; Lighthouse Keeper (Scott Copeland cover); Breakdown; Long Way Home; To Find My Love (Turner Bruton cover, Jeremy Plato singing); Constantly; Deal; Bang My Head; 17 w/Jason Boland; Fightin' For w/Mike McClure; Late Last Night (Todd Snider cover); Sick and Tired w/Gracie York; Soul Agent (Scott Evans cover, Jeremy Plato singing); On a Cloud; Wanna Rock and Roll (Ray Wylie Hubbard cover); Alabama; Stranglehold (Ted Nugent cover) w/Elle Gorman; Boys From Oklahoma (Gene Collier cover); Carney Man w/Evan Felker; Dimebag; Anywhere But Here; Don't Need You; Crazy Eddie's Last Hurrah (Reckless Kelly cover) w/Willy Braun.

Turnpike Troubadours Setlist: Night 2
Mean Old Sun; Brought Me; The Bird Hunters; Kansas City Southern; Gin, Smoke, Lies; Before the Devil Knows We're Dead; Whole Damn Town; Good Lord Lorrie; 7&7; Every Girl; The Mercury; Diamonds and Gasoline; Unrung; Tornado Warning; Pay No Rent; Long Hot Summer Day (John Hartford cover); Heaven Passing Through

NIGHT TWO

The Smokin' Oaks join Ragweed on stage Friday night.

Ryan Engleman plays guitar as Ragweed sings "Boys From Oklahoma" on Friday.

Evan Felker joins Ragweed for "Carney Man" on Friday.

Dierks and Willy Canada, on guitar and drums, play with Ragweed on Friday night.

The Mike McClure Band performs the first set on Friday night.

NIGHT TWO

Jimmy "Taco" Flex (right) and Dean Stiffler set the stage for Ragweed on Friday.

Elle Gorman joins Ragweed for "Stranglehold" on Friday.

The Turnpike Troubadours play to a full house on Friday night.

Fans light up the stadium as Turnpike sings "Diamonds and Gasoline" on Friday.

NEVER SAY NEVER

Night Three: 4.12.25

"Every day is better!" Grady Cross deadpanned from the wings as he watched the final preparations made for Cross Canadian Ragweed's third set in three nights — and first Saturday night show in nearly 15 years.

Every day of The Boys From Oklahoma also brought a completely different feeling to the artists, crew members, and 48,000 fans that filled Boone Pickens Stadium on the campus of Oklahoma State University.

In a week filled with star-studded cameos and memorable moments, Saturday still stood out. Before the stadium gates opened, Kaitlin Butts drew a crowd that, to my untrained eyes, appeared to approach 5,000 to The Midway Stage — a daytime venue across from the stadium put on by Kyle Carter and the folks behind the annual Mile 0 Fest in Key West, Florida. Later, Butts would make multiple cameos on the main stage inside the stadium as Red Dirt Woodstock hit its crescendo.

The amplified excitement can be partially attributed to a perfect Saturday in Stillwater — and, honestly, the third of four ideal spring days in north-central Oklahoma, where daytime heat gave way to a breezy night and no sign of severe weather in sight — but a trip through Gallagher-Iba Arena, OSU's basketball and wrestling arena that became the de facto artist hospitality suite for The Boys From Oklahoma, revealed plenty more reasons for enhance buzz. There was Butts, dressed like the future of country music that she is in an OSU-orange dress hand-

NIGHT THREE

made by Snake Farm Creative. There was Wyatt Flores, whose mere presence elicited whispers and corner-eye glances from anyone within his field of vision. In the Turnpike Troubadours' suite, Evan Felker held court with Molly Tuttle and Ketch Secor of Old Crow Medicine Show. I've been actively trying to avoid cliches in writing this book, but Saturday night was ... star-studded.

The first person the crowd heard from, it turns out, was Flores, who arrived in Stillwater hot from a pair of shows on Thursday and Friday nights. When The Great Divide caught wind, they asked Flores to introduce them on stage ahead of their opening set of Night 3, and the 23-year-old "Welcome to the Plains" singer obliged.

"It's nice when bands break up and then get back together, isn't it?" Mike McClure asked shortly after The Divide kicked the concert off — a reference not just to Ragweed but to high-profile breaks previously taken by the Turnpike Troubadours and The Divide itself. "We did that once, too."

Then, The Divide put on a clinic in half-hour opening sets, highlighted by the opening drumbeat of "Pour Me a Vacation" that the crowd reacted to like a call to arms, standing and cheering in unison. McClure reminded them in the lyrics, "It's Saturday night here in the big town."

Stoney LaRue was up next and earned his own gift from the crowd of undivided attention when he closed his 30 minutes with an extended jam to "Oklahoma Breakdown" before giving way to Jason Boland and The Stragglers.

It marked Boland's second night in a row of direct support to Turnpike, and, it being Saturday, he played his set to a stadium that was, for all intents and purposes, full. There were very few fans wandering in or taking their seats after Boland took the stage to "The Boys Are Back in Town" by Thin Lizzy.

With roughly two days worth of music in his catalog and only half an hour to play, Boland's show varied from night to night. Saturday, fans got to hear "Gallo del Cielo," the Tom Russell tune about an ill-fated champion fighting rooster that Joe Ely made famous and that Boland has been covering for a quarter-century.

They also got let in on a secret when Boland brought Butts on stage to join him for "If I Ever Get Back to Oklahoma" to close out his set.

NEVER SAY NEVER

"There's gonna be an album soon of people playing Stragglers tunes," Boland said, "So we'll give you a little preview here," and calling Butts to the mic.

The Turnpike Troubadours played four of the best shows of their career during The Boys From Oklahoma — the kind of shows that you'd hesitate to leave your seat to get a drink or find a restroom out of fear you'd miss something timeless or iconic. Saturday rose above the rest for Turnpike, partly because of the special moments the band had worked up for this night, and partly because Evan Felker's unbridled joy continued to spill over to band, crew and crowd.

"Me and Kyle lived here for a few years, ladies and gentlemen, and we did *not* get to play to this many people!" Felker said early in Turnpike's show, referencing the formative years in the careers of both himself and bandmate Kyle Nix, which were indeed spent in Stillwater.

As it set in that the week was more than halfway through, Felker also became vocal in calling attention to the bands that kicked the show off, telling the Saturday fans, "Give it up for Jason Boland and Stoney LaRue and The Great Divide, and all the guys who brought this music out to the world. We're very lucky to be a part of this."

He also opted to change up the words to "Whole Damn Town" again, but this time he sang, "I can sing those Wyatt Flores songs" in a bit of foreshadowing. Fans did not need to wait long for the payoff, because two songs later, Felker declared, "We are gonna get a special guest out here. He's a local guy. We're very honored to have Mr. Wyatt Flores here with us." Flores then sang the second verse and chorus of "7&7," which fans of Flores surely know is one of his favorite songs to cover at his own concerts.

But Felker's love fest only started with Flores. After that song, he said from the stage, "These shows have been my favorite shows I've ever gotten to play in my entire life," and then brought Thomas Trapp — well-known within Red Dirt circles — on stage to add guitar for "Before the Devil Knows We're Dead." He then kicked off his acoustic "Diamonds and Gasoline" with a birthday shoutout to his wife, Staci.

But it was Turnpike's last three songs of Saturday that would have had the world talking the next day if this had been their big reunion moment. First, they brought out Tuttle to cover "You're the Reason God Made Oklahoma" as a duet with Felker, while Secor joined Nix to

NIGHT THREE

give Turnpike twin fiddles to close out their third set.

But Secor also fronts Old Crow Medicine Show, and Felker is a professed fan of the band, so his presence begged the question from the sold-out stadium: *Do you think they'll play it?*

This book's editor, who had already seen the setlist by this point and already knew the answer, spoke up just before the rest of the crowd got the same answer, telling me, "I feel I must warn you that 'Wagon Wheel' is going to turn me into a different person."

She and 48,000 others, as it turned out.

Felker and Secor traded verses on "Wagon Wheel" as Boone Pickens Stadium stomped and swayed and sang along.

The thing is, though, that Turnpike has their own "Wagon Wheel," and they had it locked and loaded as soon as the Old Crow Medicine Show standby ended. When Nix, RC Edwards and Ryan Englemen hit the opening bars of "Long, Hot Summer Day," the stomping was so universally loud that fans beneath the stands in line for beer or merchandise felt the rattle from above their heads.

Between sets, the most poignant part of the entire weekend played out. Representatives from The Oklahoma Music Hall of Fame took the stage and officially inducted Cross Canadian Ragweed, The Great Divide, Jason Boland and the Stragglers, and Stoney LaRue into their membership. The Turnpike Troubadours, already members, presented the new inductees with their commemorative trophies. There was one bit of a surprise, as Shannon Canada — wife to Cody and manager to Ragweed — was also inducted for her work on the business side of Ragweed and Red Dirt.

This brings us back to Cross's remark that every day is better. Shortly after he made that comment, Ragweed took the stage to "Dead and Bloated" by the Stone Temple Pilots, and lived up to that statement from the moment they kicked off "Dimebag" and another two-plus hour set.

"Stillwater, Oklahoma!" Cody Canada said. "And, if you're not from Stillwater, Oklahoma, welcome to the greatest city in the world. We got a lot of songs to get to tonight and we're gonna play for a long time."

Early in the set, just after Canada said, "I wanna tell you a tale about the Ohio state police" and started the song "51 Pieces" — a true story of Ragweed's bus getting stopped in Ohio and law enforcement finding 51 pieces of paraphernalia inside — Canada's bravado about playing for a long time was challenged. During the first chorus of "51 Pieces," Plato's bass amp caught fire and heavy smoke billowed from behind him.

Crew and stage hands rushed to the amp before it could cause any damage, and the show went on.

Even the more normal moments that played out every night rang out a little louder on Saturday. Canada's youngest son, Willy, turned 17 earlier in the week, so every night, Cody asked the crowd to join him in singing "Happy Birthday," and the Saturday rendition happened just before Ragweed kicked off "Cry Lonely." The crowd responded with a fever pitch.

Boland returned to sing "17" for the third night in a row, just after Canada said, "Oh God, I'm getting old, people," from the mic.

Graycie York, who joined Ragweed every night of the week for a song, contributed vocals on a cover of Todd Snider's "I Believe You" on this night. McClure and Felker once again sang "Carney Man" and McClure stuck around for "Fightin' For."

Near the end of the set, when the exhausted crowd started showing their age, Canada asked, "Are you still with us? Because I'll tell Kaitlin Butts she can't come sing with us if you're not."

That remark provided the adrenaline rush the crowd needed to bring Butts up for her third appearance of the day — this time, singing the backing vocals on "Sick and Tired" which Lee Ann Womack sang on the original studio album version 20 years ago.

As she did all four nights, Charlie Cross kicked off "Boys From Oklahoma" with a harmonica intro, as a parade of artists and friends, including Flores, marched across the stage to form a backing choir for the marijuana anthem.

They kept it going through the two-song encore. First up was "Don't Need You" with Bear Plato subbing in for his father on the bass guitar.

The night ended like it began, with Wyatt Flores on stage. Flores has been covering "Alabama" in his show for the past four years, and Canada is a fan, so he asked Flores to swap verses with him on Saturday.

Just after 12:30 a.m., Ragweed ceded the stage and the house lights came back on. When The Boys From Oklahoma shows were announced,

NIGHT THREE

this was the only one planned. The music and atmosphere ensured that, while it was the third show of the weekend, it would be one that people talk about for the rest of their days.

Cross Canadian Ragweed Setlist: Night 3
Dimebag; Hammer Down; Jenny Come Back; Cry Lonely; Cold Hearted Woman; To Find My Love (Turner Bruton cover, Jeremy Plato singing); Constantly; Sister; 51 Pieces; Bang My Head; Late Last Night (Todd Snider cover); 17 w/Jason Boland; Broken; On a Cloud; Wanna Rock and Roll (Ray Wylie Hubbard cover); Carney Man w/Mike McClure and Evan Felker; Fightin' For w/Mike McClure; I Believe You (Todd Snider cover) w/Graycie York; Sick and Tired w/Kaitlin Butts; Boys from Oklahoma; Don't Need You; Alabama w/Wyatt Flores

Turnpike Troubadours Setlist: Night 3
Every Girl; Lorrie; Tornado Warning; Kansas City Southern; Whole Damn Town; Gin, Smoke, Lies; 7&7 w/Wyatt Flores; The Bird Hunters; Mean Old Sun; Before the Devil Knows We're Dead; Diamonds and Gasoline; Unrung; You're the Reason God Made Oklahoma (David Frizzell and Shelly West cover) w/Molly Tuttle; Long Hot Summer Day (John Hartford cover); Wagon Wheel (Old Crow Medicine Show cover) w/Ketch Secor

The Boone Pickens Stadium crowd during Ragweed's Saturday set.

Cody Canada wears a Mike McClure Band shirt during Ragweed's Saturday show.

Cross Canadian Ragweed's Saturday night set at The Boys From Oklahoma.

Graycie York joins Ragweed to sing "I Believe You" on Saturday night.

The crowd at The Midway Stage for Kaitlin Butts' Saturday afternoon performance.

Jason Boland and The Stragglers on stage on Saturday.

NIGHT THREE

The crowd for The Great Divide on Saturday evening.

Wyatt Flores introduces The Great Divide on Saturday.

The Turnpike Troubadours' high-energy Saturday night show.

NEVER SAY NEVER

Night Four: 4.13.25

An inadvertent consequence of Ragweed's biggest special guest on Sunday was that all but one of Ragweed's original crew members was in the stadium.

Working all week were Chris McCoy (front of house), Brian Kinzie (monitor tech), and Willard Kendall (lighting director). Meanwhile, Nathan Coit — who ran Ragweed's merch table throughout their first run as a band — attended all four shows. But it was the special guest, who we will get to momentarily, that brought former Ragweed guitar tech Joel Schoepf to Stillwater. The knock-on effect from this was a special moment as Ragweed took the stage.

As the crowd, worked over from another day of music, called for Ragweed, Kinzie ran through his pre-show routine, which entails final line checks of the stage microphones. When Kinzie got to the center mic — which Cody Canada uses — the OSU alumnus could not help himself.

"I've always wanted to say this," Kinzie said, "Herrrrre comes Bullet!"

Every Oklahoma State fan at Boone Pickens Stadium got the reference: It is the call from football public address announcer Larry Reece, introducing the Cowboys' horse-and-rider mascot, after every OSU touchdown during a home football game.

Every night Ragweed took the stage following an introduction by OSU football coach Mike Gundy. The first step in this process was

NIGHT FOUR

placing Henri Jean-Claude le Douche, Ragweed's hand-carved clown mascot, on a raised platform at the front center of the stage. This was a two-person job that fell to friends of the band. Jimmy "Taco" Flex brought Henri to his place, while either Dean Stiffler or Calvin "Doc" Plumb would follow and adorn Henri's head — the first two nights with a pair of Viking horns, and on Saturday with a custom Boys From Oklahoma Cowboy football helmet.

However, on Sunday night, Kinzie and Schoepf took on this role as Taylor Swift's "We Are Never Ever Getting Back Together" once again blared out as the band's walkout music. Kinzie placed the clown on the stage, and Schoepf followed with the football helmet. It marked the most full-circle moment of Ragweed's comeback, which had somehow managed to include all but one member of their 2000s touring party. Nine out of 10 that went free in the song "51 Pieces" were together again.

So, after Ragweed led off with "Long Way Home" — a Vietnam war lament written for Canada's father, Ronnie, who sat side stage — and Canada, decked out in a Sabrina Carpenter t-shirt, asked the crowd, "Stillwater, Oklahoma, my God, what have you done?"

He was asking rhetorically. Stillwater, Oklahoma, hadn't just brought a band back together. It brought a family back together.

Like the other four nights, it brought a day filled with music and memories to one long, drawn-out high note.

Jason Boland and The Stragglers took the stage first on Sunday, and once again varied their setlist from the night before. Boland played a cover of Jimmy LaFave's "Buffalo Return to the Plains" after shouting out the late LaFave — widely credited with making the term "Red Dirt music" stick as the genre's moniker.

Before he played his tornado tale, "Blowin' Through the Hills," Boland sent the Okies in the crowd on a scramble through their memory banks.

"I grew up in Harrah, Oklahoma, and I knew that if folks switched the channel to Channel 9, with Gary England, the shit was about to hit the fan," Boland said of the retired KWTV-TV meteorologist.

Boland ended his set, and his four-day Boys From Oklahoma run, with a cover of Bob Childers' "Outlaw Band," one of Boland's preferred set closers of his nearly 30-year career.

The Great Divide had the second set of the evening, and Mike McClure wasted no time expressing his disbelief that these shows happened at all to the 48,000-strong inside the stadium.

"I've walked out here four nights in a row, and it blows my mind every time," McClure said. "It's a long way from Boone's Farm Wine to Boone Pickens Stadium," he continued, before The Divide launched into their own tribute to Boone's Farm, "Yesterday Road."

"We're The Great Divide, and we crawled out of the early 90s to be here tonight," McClure said after the tune.

But it was McClure's bandmate, Scotte Lester, who summed up the entire weekend so concisely and thoroughly, a few songs later, that any professional journalist writing a book about the week would surely regret not coming up with it himself if he happened to be a he and his name happened to be Josh (hypothetically speaking, of course).

"Thirty years from now, people will still be talking about the Red Dirt Woodstock," Scotte said.

What the hell, man? What a line. Anyway, the title of this book is "Never Say Never" and not "Red Dirt Woodstock" and I'm sure that will be fine.

The Divide ended their week with "Mr. Devil" and a tag from "Will the Circle Be Unbroken," which Wyatt Flores joined his mentors in singing — the first of many Flores appearances on Sunday.

They were also joined late in the set by a cardboard cutout of the late Tom Skinner — mentor to McClure and co-writer of "Used to Be." The Divide turned the song into a Red Dirt anthem when they included it on their 1997 album *Break in the Storm*, and McClure has been including it in his set regularly as a tribute since Skinner's death in 2015.

Stoney LaRue played direct to the Turnpike Troubadours on Sunday, and he was similarly wistful for all that had gone on in Stillwater over four days.

"If it wasn't for these guys, I wouldn't be here," he said of The Red Dirt Rangers when he invited them on stage for "Idabel Blues."

LaRue dedicated "Down in Flames," a song he co-wrote with the late Brandon Jenkins, to members of the military.

He framed his set with "Oklahoma Breakdown" and said, "Thank you, Mike Hosty, for this song," before the final chorus.

When Turnpike took the stage for a fourth co-headlining spot in

NIGHT FOUR

four nights, frontman Evan Felker kept up the nostalgia of the first three artists.

"Sunday night crowd! This is probably the biggest Sunday night crowd I've ever played to!" he said after Turnpike opened with "Mean Old Sun" against a video backdrop of an orange-hot rising sun.

During the first verse of "Whole Damn Town," Felker sang, "I can sing those Jason Boland songs," in another nod to the opening bands and the history of Red Dirt in Stillwater.

He laid his feelings about the city bare when he wrapped up that song and said, "About half the songs that I sing tonight were written in a rented house in this town. It's amazing to be here with all you beautiful people."

After whipping the crowd into chaos with "Good Lord, Lorrie," Felker invited Flores on stage to sing "7&7" just like the previous night, telling the crowd, "We have a special guest tonight. Give it up for Red Dirt's chosen son, Wyatt Flores."

Throughout the weekend, Felker pushed himself musically, holding notes and singing way out on the edge of his vocal range, and looking comfortable throughout. All the while, Hank Early, Ryan Engleman, Kyle Nix and RC Edwards laid the groundwork and filled in the gaps around Felker's vocals with their vintage swampy, swinging version of country. They also had Bukka Allen joining them for all four shows, playing the keys and adding depth to the band's stadium sound.

When Felker and Early, for the fourth time, slowed the set down for "Diamonds and Gasoline," Felker had a request for the fans.

"I know it's been a long day ladies and gentlemen, but if your telephone still has a battery, and you have a flashlight, you would make my life a lot better," he said.

Once again, he got his wish.

"This is *the* best crowd we've ever played to," Felker said as the rest of the band filed back into place to close out the set. They were joined by Ketch Secor of Old Crow Medicine Show, who stuck around to reprise "Wagon Wheel" as he had done the night before.

"How 'bout these Boys from Oklahoma?" Secor shouted to the fans before starting the song off.

Secor stayed on stage for "Long, Hot Summer Day," making it twin fiddles with Nix as the crowd stomped, danced, and sang.

NEVER SAY NEVER

Turnpike ended with "Heaven Passing Through" off of their just-released *The Price of Admission* record.

"This is the highlight of our life and our career so far," were Felker's last words to Boone Pickens Stadium to end Turnpike's weekend run.

It was only after all that played out that Ragweed once again found themselves wrapping the night up with a rock show that lasted nearly two-and-a-half hours, with Cody Canada gushing the entire time, still in awe of the spectacle.

"A year ago I wouldn't have believed anything that any of you told me about tonight," he said on stage. "*You* have made Oklahoma music history, ladies and gentlemen."

The show itself was a mix of highlights from the entire weekend — like Graycie York joining for "I Believe You," and a stadium-wide happy birthday song for Willy Canada, and a montage of photos of the band's significant others showing behind the stage as Jeremy Plato sang "To Find My Love." Then came Elle Gorman, lead singer of Waves in April, joining for a cover of Ted Nugent's "Stranglehold" — followed by once-in-a-lifetime moments like Ragweed playing "This Time Around" for the first time during their reunion, and that special guest who brought a member of his crew, Joel Schoepf, along with him.

Parker McCollum was in fifth grade when he first heard Ragweed's music, 20 years ago. On Sunday, he got to see Ragweed play for the first time. For one song, he also got to sing *with* Ragweed, too. McCollum sang the second verse of "Constantly," while every working phone in the stadium snapped photos or snatched videos of the moment.

McCollum's own career can be traced directly to Ragweed. Shannon Canada's management partner, Robin Devin, eventually wound up managing Randy Rogers. Then, Devin and Rogers co-managed a young McCollum back before the Gold Chain Cowboy was, well, the Gold Chain Cowboy. On social media afterward, McCollum struck a heartfelt, grateful tone when he posted, "A moment I'll never forget. Thank you to those boys for having me. Long live Red Dirt music."

When McCollum returned to the wings, Ragweed pressed on, clearly not wanting the night to end. The background choir for "Boys From Oklahoma" included York and Flores, as well as Russell Doussan, the promoter responsible for the entire event. The children of Canada, Cross and Plato all got their moments on stage again, and, for the

NIGHT FOUR

fourth night in a row, a video of Ragsdale's late son, JC, playing drums, rolled on the stage backdrop as the band covered "Late Last Night" by Todd Snider.

The final song of Ragweed's main set was "Anywhere but Here," and before the song, Canada had a request for his lighting director.

"I told these guys earlier, last Saturday night I played a pool party for 45 people," he said. "Now, look what you did. Willard, light 'em up!"

Kendall responded by flooding the sold-out stadium with lights, providing one last reminder of the scale of these concerts.

The encore featured Flores returning to sing "Alabama" before McClure and Felker walked on to close out the entire weekend by taking verses on "Carney Man."

When they finished, the four members of Ragweed, plus Felker, stayed at center stage. They took bows, exchanged hugs, and waved back at the crowd of folks reluctantly, and slowly, making their way to the exits. The only question at that point was which of the five wore the biggest grin.

Then, Cross Canadian Ragweed, a band again with no sign of going anywhere other than Waco, Texas, for an encore performance in August, called it a night. The gravity of what just went down overwhelmed Canada, and he shuffled under the stage for a moment to himself. He found Ragsdale there, doing the same.

Both men embraced, and both men broke into tears.

"Why are you crying, man?" Ragsdale asked.

Canada pointed back toward the stage and stadium full of fans.

"That," he said.

Cross Canadian Ragweed Setlist: Night 4
Long Way Home; I Believe You (Todd Snider cover); 17 w/Jason Boland; Late Last Night (Todd Snider cover); Don't Need You; Bang My Head; To Find My Love (Turner Bruton cover, Jeremy Plato singing); Constantly w/Parker McCollum; Lonely Girl; Hammer Down; Sister; Soul Agent (Scott Evans cover, Jeremy Plato singing); Deal; This Time Around; Sick and Tired w/Graycie York; 42 Miles; On a Cloud; Wanna Rock and Roll (Ray Wylie Hubbard cover); Boys From Oklahoma; Stranglehold (Ted Nugent cover) w/Elle Gorman; Dimebag; Anywhere But Here; Alabama w/Wyatt Flores; Carney Man w/Mike McClure and Evan Felker.

Turnpike Troubadours Setlist: Night 4

Mean Old Sun; Brought Me; Kansas City Southern; Gin, Smoke, Lies; Before the Devil Knows We're Dead; Whole Damn Town; Good Lord Lorrie; 7&7 w/Wyatt Flores; Every Girl; The Mercury; Diamonds and Gasoline; Tornado Warning; Pay No Rent; Wagon Wheel (Old Crow Medicine Show cover) w/Ketch Secor; Long Hot Summer Day (John Hartford cover); Heaven Passing Through

Cody Canada and Randy Ragsdale embrace after the final Ragweed show. (Jamie Ragsdale)

At his first-ever Ragweed concert, Parker McCollum joins the band to sing "Constantly."

The view from the stage during "Boys From Oklahoma" on Sunday night.

Evan Felker and Cross Canadian Ragweed wave to the crowd after Sunday's show.

Cody Canada and Dierks Canada take turns on lead guitar during Ragweed's Sunday show.

NIGHT FOUR

The Great Divide play late in the day on Sunday.

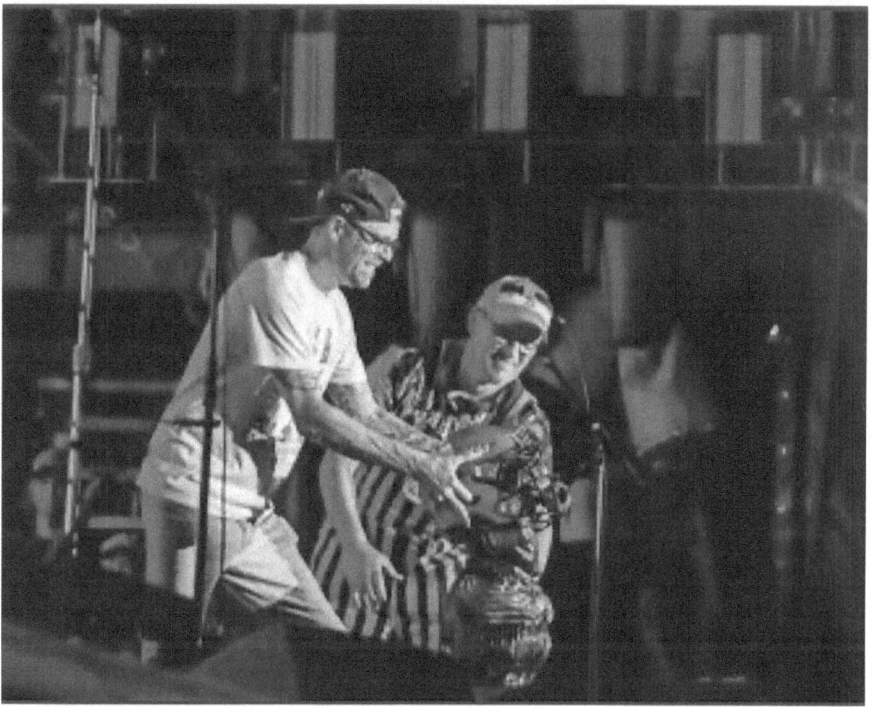

Joel Schoepf and Brian Kinzie, with Ragweed mascot Henri, set the stage Sunday. (Clay Billman)

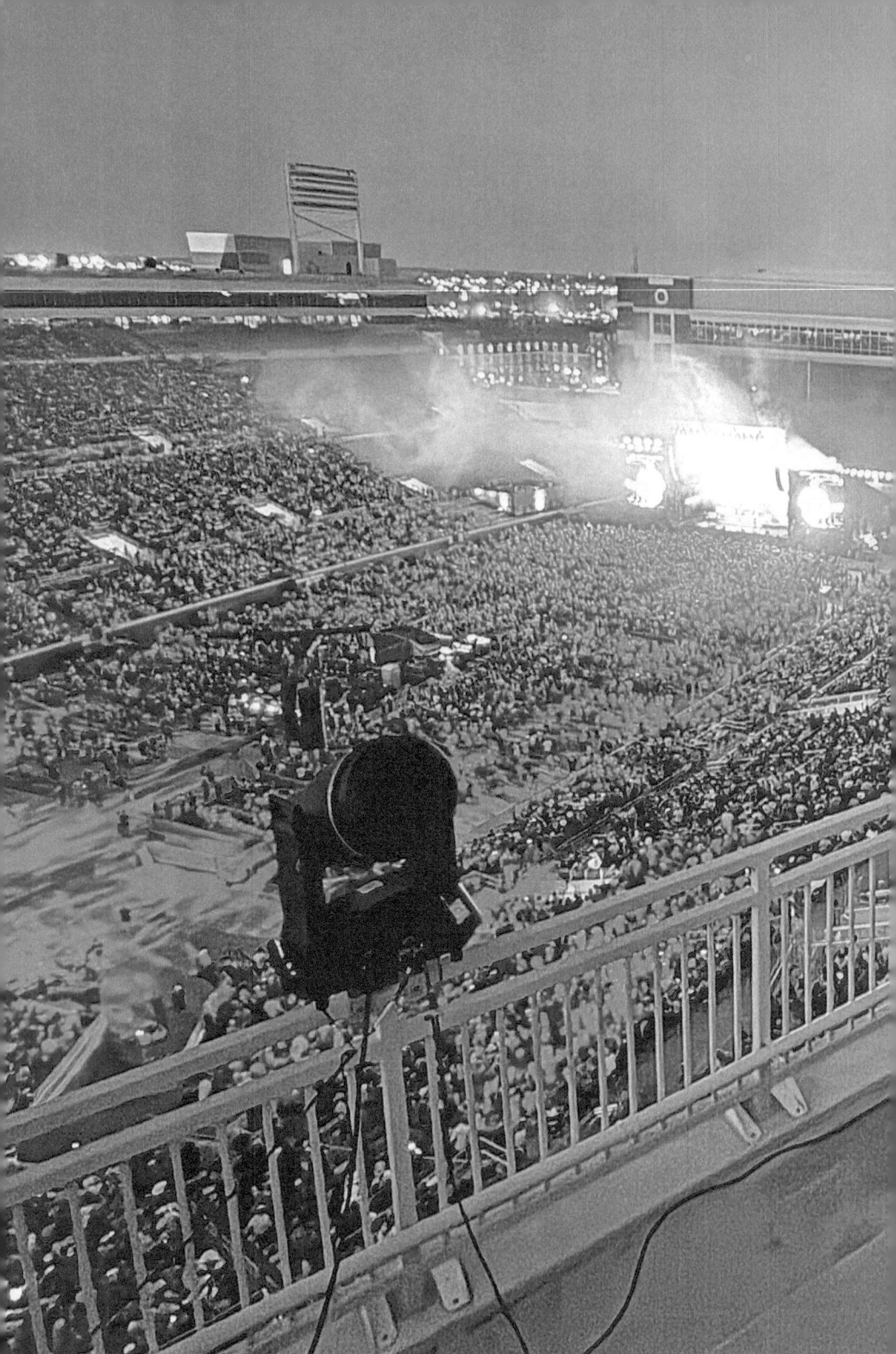
Wyatt Flores watches Turnpike from the stadium roof on Sunday night.

Ketch Secor of Old Crow Medicine Show plays with Turnpike on Sunday.

NEVER SAY NEVER

Standing in the Afterglow (the Epilogue)

What stuck out the most on The Day After was the emptiness in town. For Stillwater, and the Oklahoma State University campus, it may as well have been the dead of the winter holiday break instead of a Monday in April — both a school day and a work day in the town that had just hosted the biggest musical event Oklahoma had ever seen.

But at dusk on April 14, the town's collective hangover shone through. On The Strip, the bars were all closed, save for Willie's. On the east side of campus, one bar —George's Stables, a dive bar staple in Stillwater with a Touchtunes jukebox, a pool table, and a smoke 'em if you got 'em policy — would stay open until 2 a.m.

Whatever the individual establishments' reasons were, they would be more than justified in taking a day off. They could have run out of beer, lacked the staff to open on a Monday night after pulling, essentially, four game-day openings in a row, or simply not felt it worthwhile to unlock the doors on this night. Regardless of the answer, they had earned some rest.

Inside The Stables, only the hardest-core socialites turned out. Most of the few dozen patrons were not students, just locals passing the time on another night.

Across the street, Eskimo Joe's was open, albeit with a skeleton staff and only one of its four bars in service. Even that may have been too much, as only a handful of tables were full.

EPILOGUE

One of the full tables, though, was where Cody Canada, along with his family, some Ragweed crew members, and a handful of close friends, held court for three hours. What started as a day-after dinner turned into an evening of laughter and a heavy bar tab. The bright smiles from The Boys From Oklahoma had not waned in the slightest. They had a good night.

By the time I showed up — roughly 9 p.m. — Joe's itself was fading. I don't know when the doors closed that night, but I know it was several hours earlier than 2 a.m.

A handful of us, Canada included, decided to check out The Stables across the street. The customers already inside must have been working through their own exhaustion, because there was no mobbing Canada and no semicircle of people seeking autographs. Aside from some high-fives and offers to buy drinks, they let him unwind. After a few minutes, Canada and I found ourselves on barstools, trying to process what we had just experienced.

"Let's go," Canada said, gesturing toward the back door of the Stables.

"What?"

"Let's go outside and talk. Turn your recorder on, and let's wrap this up," and he got up and walked outside.

From the patio, you could see the still-lit Boone Pickens Stadium, where workers had been at it for 24 hours straight turning the place back into home for football. We grabbed a table, well within earshot and eyeshot of other bargoers who had opted for the patio, too. That's where we put a cap on The Boys From Oklahoma.

An August reprisal at McLane Stadium in Waco, Texas, on the campus of Baylor University, still awaits. The same folks who put on the Stillwater shows will be behind those as well. Russell Doussan and DMG are putting it on. Ragweed and Turnpike are co-headliners again. The other bands, this time, will be Shane Smith and the Saints, Wade Bowen, and American Aquarium. Bowen was a guest of Ragweed's on stage during The Boys From Oklahoma, and Smith quietly took in one of the shows from the crowd, so they know what lies in store. American Aquarium and BJ Barham will be surprised, but we already know they are going to leave all they have on stage and dare the rest of the bill to match their energy and intensity.

There's more to look forward to with Ragweed is the point. It's a complete 180 from 15 years of not knowing if there'd even be one single show to look forward to again.

All of this sank in with Canada as he and I talked and I kept the recorder running.

I let a few days pass and the euphoria — and the drinks — fade before I went back and listened. But to close out The Boys From Oklahoma, a Ragweed reunion that nobody with any serious knowledge of the band saw coming, and my fourth book, I found the best of that conversation.

Here, now, edited in the light of a clear blue morning, is Cody Canada. I'll see you all down the road.

Reflecting on the four shows:
It was four different nights, and four different experiences.

Thursday was *the* reunion, and when it was brought up that we went way over time, and we were gonna get fined, my reaction was so cocky. I didn't know what the fine would be, or if we could afford it, but I said, "We'll pay it. I don't care what the fine is, we're playing as long as we want to play."

We could have played for another hour.

The first night was the emotional night, and the rest of them felt like, "OK. We have work to do." And that's what I was hoping they would be.

On being back on stage with Ragweed:
I was running off stage after the show on the second night, and our bus driver, Nelson Reuwer, saw me in the green room — which is the OSU locker room — and he had been looking out for me all week, being really sweet and kind about everything. He saw me run into the restroom and start washing my hands.

He goes, "Dude. How did that feel?"

And I said, very loudly, "*That* is how this fucking band is supposed to sound and play. Tonight was us. Last night was the first gig back from a hiatus. Tonight was the fucking band at our best."

Then I walk back out into the locker room, and there is Ragsdale! He goes, "I heard that!"

I just went, "I'm glad you did."

EPILOGUE

We had just played in front of a lot of people, but I would have been just as happy playing that well in front of a hundred people.

Dierks Bentley came and played with us on the first night. Every night since, he's been texting me so much, telling me he has FOMO and wishes he was here. And, I guess I never realized just how big of a *fan* he is of ours. We toured together for years, and it's only just now that I see how big of a deal Ragweed is to him. That says a lot about this whole weekend.

On Ragweed's journey back:
It's cliché as fuck, but it's water under the bridge.

The thing is, the breakup was easily fixable, but we were so drunk and stoned then. To sit here and look back on this, the word is forgiveness. It's so nice to see that we have grown as people, and how much this reunion was about our kids.

There's not even a word to sum it up. This is a moment.

After the second night, we went over to Waldo's camp (the trailer where Departed and Mike McClure Band drummer Eric "Waldo" Hansen was staying), which is right next to our bus, and there was a little covey of people there. Grady walks up, and he slaps me on my stomach, and he says, "Dude! Look!" And he points at the group.

It was all of our children, sitting in a circle. Grady goes, "That's what this is."

He's right. 850,000 percent, that's what this is. This is for our children. For those kids to get up and jam, it's everything.

On what it meant to be in Stillwater again:
Man, come on. Everything about it was perfect.

Evan texted me this morning, and it said, "You revived a music scene."

I eventually wrote him back, "Well, I've been crying for 30 minutes over your text."

For Evan Felker of the Turnpike Troubadours to say that. He's my friend, and he's been my friend for 20 fucking years, but he is the Hemingway of Oklahoma music, and he's the face of it. For him to say that, out of the blue, I'm crying again thinking about it.

Here's how I sum up playing in Stillwater: Last night, we had an afterparty at Joe's for the bands, and there were cops outside the bar keeping watch. And I walked up to one of the officers and just said, "How was it?"

He said, "You want to know how many arrests I made?" And then, he held up his hands and made a zero with them.

There were a lot of drunk people, but that was it. Nobody got in fights, and nobody caused any trouble …

> At this point, we were interrupted by a patron from the next table named Rachel. I didn't ask Rachel if she worked at The Stables, but she was comfortable enough in the place that she was welcome behind the bar. She heard our conversation and wanted to add something about the good nature of the fans: "It's because everybody was so happy! They got to hear all this music, and they were happy! That's all they wanted, every day. They were just so happy to be here!"
>
> When she said that, I turned to Cody and asked, "Alright. What have you been telling me about Ragweed, going all the way back to 2015, when you started playing songs like 'Carney Man' again, and you've kept saying it to me right up until these shows began?"
>
> This was his reply:
>
> "What's wrong with making everybody happy all the time?"

EPILOGUE

Evan Felker and Mike McClure join Ragweed for "Carney Man" on Sunday night. (Clay Billman)

NEVER SAY NEVER

The Last Word

It was a cloudy day as I pulled my Honda CRV up to The Farm. I was wearing a brown tank top and an infinity scarf because it was 2013. In my pocket was a novel-sized cheat sheet text from my mom, Dana Lynn, about the history of Red Dirt music — mentioning names like Bob Childers, Mike McClure, Cross Canadian Ragweed, and Randy Crouch. She mentioned "Idabel Blues" that I was familiar with, which Stoney LaRue had recorded. She said that Stoney probably wouldn't be in attendance, but the folks that wrote it — the Red Dirt Rangers — might. She did all of this because she knew I was only 20, not old enough to have been around when all of the history of Red Dirt took place, but she didn't want me to make a fool of myself, either.

Although I don't typically get nervous around new folks, when a group of people have such an established relationship and you're the new kid walking up, I wasn't sure how I would be received. A playing circle had already formed up under the twinkle lights of a little shack, and I walked up with my guitar. I sat down in the circle, put my guitar face-down on my lap, and just listened. I wasn't about to just assume they'd let me play, but I wanted to have it out so that they knew that I *could* play.

A couple of rounds later, an older man with a fiddle, who I assumed to be Randy Crouch, based on my cheat sheet, points at me and says, "Who are you?"

I said "I'm Kaitlin Butts."

THE LAST WORD

He said, "Kaitlin, you wanna play us a song?"

I nervously said, "Sure!"

I panicked and played my song "Wild Rose." When I was finished, they all just kind of stared at me for a second, and it got quiet. Oh, God. Too much, too soon. I should have just let them play and been a wallflower.

Randy interrupted my inner self-talk and said, with a smile on his face, "Wow! Do you got another one?"

I lit up. I don't remember much after that, because I was 20 and in college with access to a cooler that no one was supervising. But I do remember the warmth, that welcome feeling that seems rare sometimes.

I always felt that in Stillwater, though. There was something about that town that, although I didn't go to school there, I felt like I was a part of it, somehow. I loved the smoky bars, the late night Dirty Curty hot dogs, and all the cowboys (a.k.a. guys who appreciated a girl who could play guitar and sing). You didn't get that down in Norman.

A couple of years later, I was attending, for the first time, The MusicFest at Steamboat. There was a pre-party downtown that Wade Bowen and Cody Canada were playing. I knew who Wade was because my friend Cale would play him and Boland on our way to my favorite line dancing bar in Tulsa — Caravan. And, I knew who Cody was because my uncle played him incessantly on the pontoon when we were out on the lake in the summertime, and I had an ex-boyfriend who said it was on his bucket list to get to smoke a joint with him. I always rolled my eyes.

We huddled into this little tiny bar — Wade and Cody on stage. The crowd knew every word. But they weren't singing rowdy songs, they were singing ballads. Really sad stuff too. I loved it. I was grabbing a drink and I heard Cody say, "I think we see a fellow Okie in the crowd tonight. Kaitlin Butts. Kaitlin Butts? Would you wanna come sing something?"

Am I hallucinating? Did they just say my name? I've never met these men in my life. Did they just say my name? How do they know my name? Or my face?

I start getting pushed up to the front. *What is happening?*

Cody hands me his low-hanging guitar and a pick and heads to the bar for a drink. I'm standing up there with Wade Bowen, completely

NEVER SAY NEVER

shell-shocked, not knowing what to play. I quickly decide on a crowd favorite, "Folsom Prison Blues."

When I got off stage, I was still so confused. How did Cody know I was there or who I even was to begin with? It's still a mystery to me to this day. But, I quickly learned that this is just what they do.

Everyone's there to see them play their songs, but they pull up the next guy — or in this case, girl — in line and give them their Red Dirt stamp of approval and welcome them into their circle and in front of their audience. They don't care if you're green and unpolished or radio-ready. They care about songs and giving a hand to the next generation. That's who they are, and it's because of where they come from and who helped pull them up, too.

Kaitlin Butts, April 2025

THE LAST WORD

APPENDIX

Back Lounge Publishing

Read More from the Author

Learn more about Red Dirt (2020), The Motel Cowboy Show (2023), and Red Dirt Unplugged (2024) at backloungepublishing.com

Rolling Stone Stories Referenced

All Rolling Stone pieces cited in Never Say Never can be found at rollingstone.com/author/josh-crutchmer

Official Never Say Never Playlists

Visit the links atop backloungepublishing.com/media for the Apple Music and Spotify playlists.

Books

Dirt & Spirit: A History of the Red Dirt Music Scene Vol. 1., by Tonya Little (2025) | littleokieland.com

Her Country: How the Women of Country Music Became the Success They Were Never Supposed to Be, by Marissa Moss (2022)

Newsletters and Patreons

Don't Rock the Inbox, by Natalie Weiner and Marissa Moss | dontrocktheinbox.substack.com

Time & Temperature with Rhett Miller | rhettmiller.substack.com

American Aquarium Patreon | patreon.com/c/americanaquarium

Documentary

Oklahoma Breakdown: The Mike Hosty Story | oklahomabreakdown.com

Media

The Back Lounge Youtube: www.youtube.com/@RedDirtBook

Loose Ends

As of this writing, I intend to keep all of my books housed under the completely made-up Back Lounge Publishing imprint. Find it at backloungepublishing.com. You can contact me that way as well.

Find my *New York Times* work by visiting nytimes.com/search and searching my name.

Currently, you can connect with me on Bluesky and Instagram by searching my name. (It is easy, as I am the

APPENDIX

Welcome to the Back Lounge

crutchmer.com

I am creating a new, independent online home for my music work in 2025. This will be a hub for stories, podcasts, events and newsletters, as well as your chance to reach me directly and help shape the direction of my coverage of independent music (don't worry, my New York Times and Rolling Stone work is going nowhere — this project aims to make all of that easier).

$5 from every book sold at neversayneverbook.com and 10% of Amazon royalties through November 30, 2025, will benefit the Okmulgee Family YMCA

This is a homecoming concert, and I would like to share this book with the first nonprofit I was ever a part of in my hometown. Your purchase will have a direct impact, contributing to support, memberships, jerseys and more for youth sports as well as families in need of care.

ymcatulsa.org/okmulgee

Index

A

A Cat in the Rain (album) 30, 31, 34
Alabama (song) 38, 144, 165
Aldean, Jason 16, 20
Allen, Bukka 26, 163
American Aquarium 181, 192
Austin, TX 43

B

Bang My Head (song) 103, 123, 124, 145, 165
Barham, BJ 181
Baylor University 181
Before the Devil Knows We're Dead 104, 122, 124, 142, 145, 166
Be Here (song) 30, 33, 35
Bentley, Dierks 38, 103, 104, 112, 183
Beyoncé 24
Billman, Clay 68, 98, 112, 175
Billy Bob's Texas 49, 54, 79
Bingham, Ryan 25, 26
The Bird Hunters (song) 104, 122, 124, 145
Blowin' Through the Hills (song) 161
Boland, Jason 6, 7, 8, 18, 36, 37, 38, 42, 43, 44, 46, 48, 49, 50, 56, 61, 101, 102, 103, 104, 121, 122, 123, 124, 141, 142, 143, 144, 145, 156, 161, 163, 165, 189

Boone Pickens Stadium 4, 6, 15, 18, 19, 20, 25, 62, 73, 81, 92, 95, 99, 101, 102, 110, 120, 121, 140, 143, 146, 160, 162, 164, 181
Bowen, Wade 5, 103, 181, 189
The Boys From Oklahoma 4, 6, 7, 14, 15, 16, 18, 20, 22, 24, 26, 30, 36, 43, 44, 45, 48, 50, 54, 82, 92, 93, 100, 101, 114, 120, 140, 142, 144, 150, 181, 182
Boys From Oklahoma (song) 73, 103, 123, 128, 144, 164, 170
Braun Brothers Reunion 5
Braun, Cody 103
Braun, Willy 103, 123, 124
Break in the Storm (album) 162
The Brooklyn Kid (song) 26, 103, 104, 123
Brooks, Garth 25
Bryan, Zach 34
Buffalo Return to the Plains (song) 43, 161
Burke, Johnny 25
Butts, Kaitlin 8, 30, 140, 141, 142, 144, 145, 154, 188, 189, 190

C

Cain's Ballroom 7, 25, 49, 76, 84, 94
Calf Fry 101
Canada, Cody 5, 6, 7, 14, 36, 42, 48, 50, 52, 56, 61, 62, 63, 70, 73, 74, 76, 79, 86,

INDEX

90, 92, 95, 96, 98, 99, 100, 120, 143, 148, 160, 164, 167, 174, 181, 182, 189
Canada, Dierks 8, 16, 72, 92, 94, 132, 174
Canada, Ronnie 161
Canada, Shannon 5, 20, 64, 93, 143, 164
Canada, Willy 8, 16, 72, 92, 104, 132, 144, 164
Carney Man (song) 26, 103, 123, 124, 130, 144, 145, 165, 184
Carpenter, Sabrina 161
Carter, Kyle 8, 94, 140
Chainsaw Kittens 58
Chicago 14, 63, 78
Childers, Bob 26, 37, 48, 49, 65, 161, 188
Clark, Guy 37
Clark, Stan 8
Coachella 15, 16, 19, 20
Cody Canada and The Departed 5, 6, 7, 14, 15, 17, 63, 81, 86, 88, 90, 92, 96, 120
Coit, Nathan 160
Collier, Gene 103, 104, 123, 124
Constantly (song) 38, 103, 164, 168
Conway, Bryce 36
Crazy Eddie's Last Hurrah (song) 103, 104, 123, 124
Cross Canadian Ragweed 4, 5, 6, 7, 11, 12, 14, 15, 16, 17, 18, 19, 20, 22, 24, 25, 26, 30, 36, 37, 38, 39, 42, 43, 45, 49, 56, 60, 62, 63, 64, 65, 70, 71, 72, 73, 78, 79, 80, 81, 82, 84, 86, 87, 88, 92, 93, 94, 95, 99, 100, 101, 102, 103, 106, 108, 110, 122, 123, 124, 126, 128, 130, 132, 135, 140, 141, 143, 144, 145, 146, 148, 150, 152, 160, 161, 164, 165, 167, 168, 172, 174, 175, 181, 182, 183, 184, 188
Cross Canadian Ragweed (The Purple Album) 62, 71
Cross, Charlie 16, 72, 73, 102, 144
Cross, Grady 6, 16, 62, 64, 70, 72, 74, 76, 78, 80, 87, 95, 99, 101, 123, 140, 183
Cross, Robin 73
Cross, Slaid 16, 70, 72, 73, 74, 123
Crouch, Rand 48, 188
Crutchmer, Josh 62, 192
Crutchmer, Wes 8, 64
Cry Lonely (song) 104, 144, 145

D

Daddy's at Home (song) 82
The Daily O'Collegian 63, 65
Dale, Katie 8
Damn Quails 120
Dead and Bloated (song) 143
Dedringers 26
The Deli 55, 57, 58
Diamonds and Gasoline (album and song) 31, 34, 104, 122, 124, 138, 142, 145, 163, 166
Dimebag (song) 124, 143, 145, 165
Don't Need You (song) 104, 123, 124, 144, 145, 165
Doussan Music Group 15, 20, 181
Doussan, Russell 8, 15, 18, 164, 181
Down in Flames (song) 49, 121, 162
Downtown (album) 49
Dyer, William 4, 5

E

Eady, Jason 25
Earle, Steve 37, 44
Early, Hank 26, 122, 163
Edwards, RC 26, 31, 35, 143, 163
Engleman, Ryan 26, 128, 163
Eskimo Joe's 7, 8, 18, 48, 63, 74, 81, 98, 120, 180
Evan Felker and Friends 26

F

The Farm 37, 48, 188
Feet Don't Touch The Ground (song) 49
Felker, Evan 5, 6, 8, 11, 24, 25, 26, 27, 31, 55, 71, 102, 103, 104, 122, 123, 124, 130, 141, 142, 143, 144, 145, 163, 164, 165, 172, 183
Felker, Staci 142
51 Pieces (song) 143, 144, 145, 161
Fightin' For (song) 124, 144, 145
Fitzpatrick, Christopher 55, 56
Flaming Lips 58
Fleming, Nate 64
Flex, Jimmy "Taco" 8, 67, 94, 135, 161

INDEX

Flex, Kari 8, 94
Flores, Wyatt 4, 5, 8, 12, 30, 54, 141, 142, 144, 145, 157, 162, 163, 164, 165, 176
Folk, Jon 8, 15, 17, 18, 25, 72, 73, 81, 93
Fort Worth, TX 25, 38, 59, 95
Fullbright, John 31

G

Gallagher-Iba Arena 15, 19, 20, 140
Gallo del Cielo (song) 141
Gamble, Al 55
Gamble Brothers Band 55
Gamble, Chad 55
George's Stables 180
Good Lord Lorrie (song) 102, 104, 124, 166
Gorman, Elle 124, 135, 164, 165
Grady's 66 Pub 72
Grady's Green Room 72
The Great Divide 6, 7, 8, 10, 11, 15, 18, 24, 36, 37, 38, 39, 40, 43, 45, 71, 101, 102, 115, 120, 121, 141, 142, 143, 157, 162, 175
Green, Kelley 10, 36
Gundy, Mike 99, 100, 160

H

Hall, Tom T. 44
Hancock, Andrea 8, 63, 65
Hansen, Eric "Waldo" 14, 120, 183
Hartford, John 102, 104, 124, 145, 166
Henri Jean-Claude le Douche 161, 175
High Times and Hangovers tours 103
Highway 377 (album) 63, 65, 82
Hillhouse, Lori 8
Holland, Tim 8
Hosty Duo 55, 59
Hosty, Mike 49, 54, 55, 56, 57, 58, 59, 60, 61, 101, 162, 192
Hosty Trio 55, 56, 57, 58, 61
Hudak, Joe 8

I

I am Not Broken (song) 121

I Believe You (song) 144, 145, 152, 164, 165
Idabel Blues (song) 101, 162, 188
If I Ever Get Back to Oklahoma (song) 121, 141
Isbell, Jason 55, 61

J

Jackson, Alan 16
Jason Boland and The Stragglers 6, 42, 101, 121, 141, 156, 161
Jason Isbell and The 400 Unit 55
Jay, Neil 80
Jenkins, Brandon 25, 48, 65, 162
Jennings, Shooter 8, 30, 31, 32, 34
JJ's Alley 55
Joe's on Weed Street 14
Joe's On Weed Street 63
Joe State Tailgate 63, 74, 81
Johnny's Song (song) 82
Jolly, Tom 8
Jordan, Eli 102

K

Kazoo 55
Keen, Robert Earl 15, 37
Keith, Braxton 44
Keith, Toby 54
Kendall, Willard 8, 103, 160, 165
Key West, FL 7, 52, 70, 72, 81, 95, 140
Kinzie, Brian 8, 160, 161, 175
Kirkley, Ashley 8

L

LaFave, Jimmy 43, 161
Lambert, Miranda 16, 20
Larry Joe Taylor Festival 61
LaRue, Stoney 6, 7, 8, 26, 36, 37, 43, 48, 49, 50, 52, 54, 56, 60, 80, 101, 104, 114, 121, 141, 142, 143, 162, 188
The Last Kings of Babylon (album) 43, 121
Late Last Night (song) 104, 124, 145, 165
Lester, JJ 36, 55

INDEX

Lester, Scotte 10, 36, 162
Live at Billy Bob's (album) 49, 54
Long, Hot Summer Day (song) 102, 143, 163
Lopez, Annemarie 8
Lopez, Jake 8

M

McClure, Mike 11, 15, 36, 37, 38, 39, 49, 101, 103, 104, 120, 121, 123, 124, 134, 141, 144, 145, 148, 162, 165, 183, 188
McCollum, Parker 164, 165, 168
McCoy, Chris 8, 100, 160
McDaniel, Marci 8
McElhaney, Katie 8
McInnes, Andrew 8
McLane Stadium 181
Mean Old Sun (song) 104, 116, 122, 124, 145, 163, 166
Meloy, Josh 30
Mendez, Jeanette 21
The Meters 57
Mike McClure Band 120, 121, 134, 148, 183
Mile 0 Fest 7, 52, 70, 81, 87, 95, 140
Milford, Braden 5
Mr. Devil (song) 162

N

New Braunfels, TX 6, 16
The New York Times 6, 8, 192, 193
Next to Last Hank Williams (song) 43, 44, 121
Nirvana 25, 56, 58
Nix, Kyle 25, 26, 31, 62, 142, 143, 163
Nixons 58
Noel, Mark 8
Nothing You Can Do (song) 31
Number (song) 70, 72, 123
Nunn, Gary P. 37

O

Okemah, OK 31
Oklahoma Breakdown (song) 49, 50, 54, 55, 56, 60, 61, 101, 121, 141, 162, 192

Oklahoma Breakdown: The Mike Hosty Story 55, 192
Oklahoma City 48, 55, 72, 73
Oklahoma International Bluegrass Festival 26
Oklahoma Music Hall of Fame 7, 43, 95, 101, 143
Oklahoma State Univesity 4, 15, 19, 20, 48, 62, 63, 64, 74, 81, 88, 95, 99, 100, 102, 120, 140, 160, 180
Okmulgee Family YMCA 8, 193
Okmulgee, OK 8, 12, 193
Old Crow Medicine Show 4, 31, 32, 141, 143, 145, 163, 166, 178
On a Cloud (song) 26, 38, 62, 63, 64, 65, 66, 67, 68, 104, 124, 145, 165
One Chord Song (song) 49, 121
On the Red River (song) 31
Organic Boogie Band 49
Out in the Fields (song) 121
Outlaw Band (song) 161

P

Pantera 123
Parks, Sam 26
Pay (song) 38
Pearl Snaps (song) 44, 101
Pearson, Gabe 26
Peso in My Pocket (album) 54
Phillips, Bo 25
Phillips, C.J. 50, 121
Plato, Bear 123, 144
Plato, Jeremy 6, 14, 62, 86, 90, 99, 101, 103, 124, 145, 164, 165
Plumb, Calvin "Doc" 161
Pour Me a Vacation (song) 141
The Price of Admission (album) 30, 31, 102, 164
Providence (album) 39
Purifoy, Todd 22

R

Ragsdale, Jamie 80, 167
Ragsdale, JC 65, 79, 80, 81, 82, 95
Ragsdale, Johnny C. 65, 70, 79

INDEX

Ragsdale, Julia 80
Ragsdale, Mandi 65, 82
Ragsdale, Randy 6, 16, 62, 64, 70, 78, 84, 87, 99, 101, 123, 167
Ragsdale, Ruth Ann 82
Reckless Kelly 103, 104, 123, 124
Red Dirt Album 49
Red Dirt Music 4, 18, 38, 48, 60, 71, 99, 100, 161, 164, 188
Red Dirt Rangers 37, 101, 103, 123, 162, 188
Red Dirt Relief Fund 8
Red Dirt Unplugged (book) 5, 6, 7
Red Rocks Amphitheatre 94
Reece, Larry 81, 160
Reed, Brandy 8
Remember The Ten 64
Reuwer, Nelson 8, 182
Rinella, Steve 32
Roark, Lance 31
Rolling Stone 6, 7, 8, 14, 15, 17, 55, 65, 94, 192, 193
Rosalie (dog) 94
Ruby Ann (song) 31

S

Sacks, Carla 8
Scace, Paddy 8
Schoepf, Joel 160, 161, 164, 175
Schoepf, Robin Devin 164
Secor, Ketch 4, 31, 32, 141, 142, 143, 145, 163, 166, 178
7&7 (song) 104, 124, 142, 145, 163, 166
17 (song) 12, 103, 123, 144
Shane Smith and the Saints 181
Shirtum, Caleb 120
Shortcakes Diner 123
Shrum, Darren 8, 15, 16, 19
Shrum, Kayse 15, 19, 21, 65, 81, 88
Sick and Tired (song) 104, 124, 144, 145, 165
Simonett, Dave 31, 32
Sisioan, Allie 8
Sivick, Joe 8
Skinner, Tom 26, 65, 162

Smokin' Oaks 16, 70, 123, 126
Snider, Todd 104, 124, 144, 145, 165
Soul Gravy (album) 6, 71
Spatz, Tony 26
Springsteen, Bruce 79
Stephenville, TX 37, 61
Stiffler, Dean 8, 135, 161
Stiffler, Merylee 8
Stillwater, OK 4, 7, 10, 12, 14, 18, 24, 25, 26, 30, 36, 37, 38, 42, 43, 44, 48, 49, 58, 63, 65, 66, 70, 92, 93, 98, 99, 101, 102, 120, 121, 122, 123, 140, 141, 142, 143, 160, 161, 162, 163, 180, 181, 183, 189
Stone, Shelby 104
Stone Temple Pilots 143
Sugar Free All-Stars 55
Suicide Blues (song) 123
Sunset Sound Studio 3 31, 34
Swift, Taylor 24, 100, 161

T

Tahlequah, OK 32
Texas Moon (song) 49
Toadies 95
Top, Zach 44
Trampled by Turtles 31, 32
Trapp, Thomas 26, 142
Tulsa, OK 7, 25, 43, 49, 58, 59, 76, 94, 121, 189
Tulsa Time (song) 121
Tumbleweed Dance Hall 37, 101, 120
The Turnpike Troubadours 4, 5, 8, 11, 12, 15, 18, 21, 24, 25, 26, 28, 30, 31, 34, 35, 36, 42, 55, 61, 62, 71, 93, 94, 101, 102, 104, 116, 118, 121, 122, 124, 136, 138, 141, 142, 143, 145, 158, 162, 163, 164, 166, 176, 178, 181, 183
Tuttle, Molly 4, 141, 142, 145

U

Universal South 25, 71
Used to Be (song) 162

V

Vaughn, Kaylee 8
The Void (song) 121

W

Waco, TX 165, 181
Wagon Wheel (song) 143, 145, 163, 166
Wakeland 58
Walk (song) 123
Waters, Kyle 8, 15, 19, 94
Waters, Trey 16
Waves in April 16, 92, 164
We Are Never Ever Getting Back Together (song) 100, 161
Weiberg, Chad 8
Welcome to the Plains (album) 12, 141
White, Jack 61
Willie's Saloon 48
Will the Circle Be Unbroken (song) 162
WME 25
Womack, Lee Ann 144
Wormy Dog Saloon 16, 38, 48, 61, 63, 65, 66, 79, 100
Wright, Kenyatta 15

Y

Yellow House 48, 49, 50
Yesterday Road (song) 162
Yoakam, Dwight 44
York, Graycie 104, 144, 145, 152, 164, 165
Young, Lola 50
You're the Reason God Made Oklahoma (song) 142, 145
Yukon, OK 16, 36, 70, 72, 80, 87

Z

Zagata, Andrea 8

About the Author

Josh Crutchmer is the planning editor at *The New York Times*. Mr. Crutchmer is responsible for the organization of the daily newspaper as well as the look and content of *The Times*' front page — and he gets the occasional byline. Prior to joining *The Times*, he was the assistant managing editor of *The Plain Dealer* in Cleveland where, among other high-profile events, he oversaw coverage and production of the annual Rock & Roll Hall of Fame inductions. Previously, he has worked at *The Chicago Tribune*, *The Buffalo News*, the *Minneapolis Star Tribune*, the *Omaha World-Herald*, *The Arizona Republic*, and *The Oklahoman*.

He has a long history in music journalism, even prior to writing *Red Dirt*. He was tapped to write obituaries for Merle Haggard and George Jones for *The Plain Dealer* and *Nashville City Paper*, respectively. He covered the rise to prominence of Cross Canadian Ragweed for *The Oklahoman* and the band's final show in 2010 for an entertainment arm of *The Chicago Tribune*.

During the process of writing *Red Dirt Unplugged*, Crutchmer also chronicled Wyatt Flores's 2024 mental health break in a *New York Times* profile, and later stumbled upon the news of The Boys From Oklahoma concerts and 2025 Cross Canadian Ragweed reunion — breaking that news with an exclusive interview in *Rolling Stone*.

A native Oklahoman and graduate of Oklahoma State University, Mr. Crutchmer has had a close relationship to the state's Red Dirt Music scene since 2000. His experience in Red Dirt extends not just to the artists but to the crew members, sound engineers, bar owners and tour managers behind the scenes whose efforts define what it means to live and work with a love of music.

www.ingramcontent.com/pod-product-compliance
Lightning Source LLC
Chambersburg PA
CBHW032135250426
43661CB00077B/2131